The One-Stop Guide to Jesus

THE
ONE-STOP
Guide to
Jesus

Mike Beaumont

LION

A Lion Book
an imprint of
Lion Hudson plc
Wilkinson House, Jordan Hill Road,
Oxford OX2 8DR, England
www.lionhudson.com

ISBN 978 0 7459 5361 8

Distributed by:
UK: Marston Book Services, PO Box 269, Abingdon, Oxon, OX14 4YN
USA: Trafalgar Square Publishing, 814 N. Franklin Street, Chicago, IL 60610
USA Christian Market: Kregel Publications, PO Box 2607, Grand Rapids,
Michigan 49501

First edition 2010
10 9 8 7 6 5 4 3 2 1 0

Acknowledgments
Scripture quotations (except those listed below) are taken from the *Holy Bible, New
International Version*, copyright © 1973, 1978, 1984 International Bible Society.
Used by permission of Zondervan and Hodder & Stoughton Limited. All rights
reserved. The 'NIV' and 'New International Version' trademarks are registered in
the United States Patent and Trademark Office by International Bible Society.
Use of either trademark requires the permission of International Bible Society. UK
trademark number 1448790. p. 19: scripture quotation is from the *Good News Bible*
published by The Bible Societies/HarperCollins Publishers, copyright © 1966, 1971,
1976, 1992 American Bible Society. p. 21: scripture quotation is taken from the *Holy
Bible, New Living Translation*, copyright © 1996. Used by permission of Tyndale
House Publishers, Inc., Wheaton, Illinois 60189. All rights reserved. p. 31: scripture
quotation is from the *Contemporary English Version* published by The Bible
Societies/HarperCollins Publishers, copyright © 1991, 1992, 1995 American Bible
Society.
p. 71: scripture quotation is taken from the *Holy Bible, New Living Translation*,
copyright © 1996. Used by permission of Tyndale House Publishers, Inc., Wheaton,
Illinois 60189. All rights reserved. p. 79: scripture quotation is taken from the *New
King James Version* copyright © 1982, 1979 by Thomas Nelson, Inc.

A catalogue record for this book is available
from the British Library

Typeset in News 702 BT and Humanist 777 BT
Printed and bound in Singapore

Contents

Introduction

Probably no one in history has fascinated people more, attracted people more, inspired people more, yet also angered people more, than Jesus. Born into an ordinary Jewish family living in a tiny Middle-Eastern state under cruel military occupation, Jesus spent his first thirty years in the shadows, doing what we all do – working, eating, laughing, sleeping and, because he was a good Jewish boy, worshipping God. But then one day he burst from those shadows onto the public scene, claiming God's kingdom had arrived and calling people to a radical way of living. He caused turmoil (for good or bad, depending how you saw it) wherever he went, until finally, the authorities had had enough and summarily executed him in the most shameful way known in his day.

And that, all else being equal, would have been that. Except it wasn't. Three days later his followers were yanked from dark despair and were telling everybody Jesus was alive, risen from the dead. They claimed he spent forty days with them, until he was dramatically taken up into heaven from where he sent his Holy Spirit to them ten days later. Within just twenty years his followers had taken this message to every major city of the Roman empire, as well as Africa and India. Today his followers number over 2 billion, one-third of the world's population. And all this from a man whose work spanned just three years in an obscure part of the Middle East, and who never wrote a book or had a TV programme.

So what brought this about? What changed those first disciples? They would have said that it was, quite simply, Jesus, whom they came to see as more than they had ever imagined: not just a prophet or religious teacher, but no one less than God himself.

This book explores what the Bible says about this man Jesus. It assumes no prior knowledge on the reader's part and is written in non-technical language, making it ideal for those wishing to explore Christianity or who are new to it – though its approach and presentation will hopefully bring a fresh angle for long-term followers too. All I try to do is unpack in a thematic way what the New Testament says about, and claims for, this man against the background of his time. By the end of the book, I hope you will have got a fair idea of the essence of this man Jesus: what he said, what he did, why he did it, who he thought he was, and what he was like – *amazingly kind*, especially to people who didn't expect it or necessarily deserve it, because he himself was convinced that this was what God is really like.

Whether you are exploring Christianity or have been a follower of Jesus for many years, my hope is that *The One-Stop Guide to Jesus* will help you in your journey of discovering more about the one whom Christians claim was God – a kind and gracious God – who came, and still comes, among us.

Mike Beaumont,
Oxford

His Story
LOOKING FOR JESUS

For the past 2,000 years, people have been telling the story of Jesus. Indeed, no matter how Christianity has been expressed, in different times and cultures, the focus has always been on *him*. While other movements and '-isms' can survive without their founder, Christianity cannot. Indeed, if it could be proved that Jesus never existed at all, Christianity would collapse; for Christianity *is* Christ. If Jesus goes, everything goes with him; for Christianity is not about a teaching, but about a person.

Can We Find the Real Jesus?

Because Jesus lived so long ago, can we ever really know what he was like? Can we ever find the real Jesus? Scholars' quest for the historical Jesus (as it became known) began over 250 years ago through a renewed interest in studying ancient documents that was sparked off by the Enlightenment. At first, the more they studied, the more they doubted, leaving little of the miraculous Jesus of the Gospels. However, more recent discoveries and study of contemporary Jewish writings, like the Dead Sea Scrolls, has shown that the Bible's account of Jesus fits in exactly with what we now know of life, thought and beliefs in first-century Judaism. We can now be more certain than ever that the picture of Jesus in the Gospels is highly trustworthy and provides a solid basis for a modern-day search for Jesus.

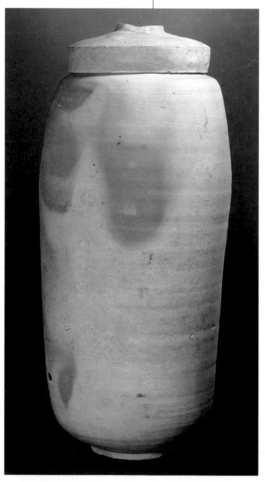

A large first-century terracotta jar of the kind in which the Dead Sea Scrolls were hidden. Discovered accidentally in 1947 by Bedouin shepherds, the jars contained nearly 900 scrolls of religious documents and copies of the Old Testament that had been hidden in caves near Qumran by the Essenes to protect them during the Jewish–Roman war of AD 66–70.

Evidence for Jesus' Life

While the main evidence for Jesus' life comes from the four Gospels and earlier oral traditions noted in New Testament letters (e.g. 1 Corinthians 15:3–8), there is also important and impartial evidence through the Roman historian Josephus (c. AD 37–100). Coming from a Jewish priestly family and for a period governor of Galilee (where Jesus lived), he was captured by the Romans during the Jewish war of AD 66–70 and spent the rest of his life as advisor and historian to three emperors, Vespasian, Titus and Domitian. His writings provide invaluable non-Christian eyewitness testimony to Christianity in the first century. While there are some hesitancies over the exact wording of his comments on Jesus, their existence at the very least demonstrates Jesus' historicity.

Jesus and the Bigger Picture

For Christians, the story of Jesus isn't separate from the Old Testament's story; rather, it is the key to understanding it, for Jesus claimed both to fulfil its promises to the Jews and to launch the next phase of God's rescue plan for all nations. It often helps us to understand the New Testament better by providing the background to what Jesus said or did; and in fact, ignoring it invariably leads to a wrong understanding of Jesus.

'Nazareth! Can anything good come from there?' Nathanael asked. 'Come and see,' said Philip.

JOHN 1:46

● SEE ALSO
HIS BIOGRAPHERS PP. 10–11
HIS NATION PP. 16–17
QUMRAN P. 18

Other Evidence for Jesus

Non-Jewish:

■ Mara ben Serapion, Syrian philosopher, c. AD 73: 'What advantage did the Jews gain from executing their wise king? It was just after that their kingdom was abolished… Nor did the wise king die for good; he lived on in the teaching which he had given.'

■ Tacitus, Roman historian, c. AD 110: 'Christus, from whom the name [Christian] had its origin, suffered the extreme penalty during the reign of Tiberius at the hands of one of our procurators, Pontius Pilatus, and a most mischievous superstition, thus checked for the moment, again broke out not only in Judea, the first source of the evil, but even in Rome.'

Jewish:

■ In the Talmud (Jewish commentary) the rabbis hoped that 'they did not have a son or disciple who taught heresy like Jesus the Nazarene'.

■ 'On the eve of Passover they hanged Jesus the Nazarene… Jesus the Nazarene practised magic and led Israel astray' *(Sanhedrin)*.

Qur'an:

■ Jesus is mentioned several times in Islam's holy book, the Qur'an.

Bust of Josephus, who wrote in his *Antiquities* of the Jews: 'Now there was about this time Jesus, a wise man, if it be lawful to call him a man; for he was a doer of wonderful works, a teacher of those who receive the truth gladly. He won over many Jews and many Gentiles. He was the Christ. And when Pilate, at the suggestion of the leading men amongst us, had condemned him to the cross, those that loved him at the first did not forsake him; for he appeared to them alive again the third day, for God's prophets had prophesied these and ten thousand other wonderful things about him. And the tribe of Christians, so called after him, are not extinct at this day.'

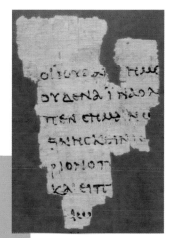

The earliest known fragment of the New Testament, dating from around AD 125. It is part of John, chapter 18.

COMPARISON OF THE GOSPELS AND OTHER ANCIENT TEXTS

This chart shows how there is far more, and far earlier, evidence for the life of Jesus than any other event of ancient history. The figures given are solely for New Testament manuscripts in Greek; if we add early copies in Syriac, Latin, Coptic and Aramaic, then the total number comes to around 24,000.

	Date of original document	Date of oldest surviving copy	Time gap	Number of ancient copies
Thucydides *History of the Peloponnesian War*	430–400 BC	AD 900	1,300 years	8
Caesar *Gallic Wars*	52–51 BC	AD 850	900 years	10
Tacitus *Histories*	AD 104–109	AD 800	700 years	2
Matthew, Mark, Luke, John *The Four Gospels*	AD 65–90	AD 350 (whole) AD 200 (much) AD 125 (fragment)	260–285 years 110–135 years 35 years	c. 2,350 (Gospels) c. 5,500 (New Testament)

KEY SAYING

'Seek and you will find.'

MATTHEW 7:7

His Biographers
EXPLAINING JESUS

To call the Gospel writers Jesus' biographers isn't really the right word. After all, so much is missing – his appearance, upbringing, education, work – everything we might reasonably expect in a modern biography. And not only are things omitted, there is a disproportionate focus on the last week of his life (one-third of Mark, one-half of John). Clearly their purpose, then, was far more than just telling a story; it was sharing good news.

This carving over the door of the Church of St Trophime at Arles represents an understanding of the emphasis of each of the Gospels. Clockwise from top left, it portrays Jesus as: a man (Matthew), reflecting Jesus' humanity; an eagle (John), reflecting Jesus' anointing by the Spirit; an ox (Luke), reflecting Jesus' sacrifice; a lion (Mark), reflecting Jesus' royalty.

Good News

Of the twenty-seven books in the New Testament, four are called 'Gospels'. Gospel (in Greek, *euangelion*) means 'good news'. Although now a religious word, it originally had a secular meaning. Whenever the emperor had news, he sent messengers across his empire to town squares where they shouted, '*Euangelion!*', and everyone came running to find out more.

No book had ever been called a '*euangelion*' before; but there was simply no literary category for what these writers wanted to say about Jesus. It was history, biography, memoirs, sayings – all this, but more; and so they created a new genre, reflecting that here was unashamed, impassioned 'good news' about Jesus that was worth listening to. But because good news isn't good news unless it's true, they were also concerned to give an accurate picture of what really happened.

Part of the Gospel of Thomas, a collection of sayings in Coptic, discovered in Nag Hammadi in Egypt in 1945. Containing no narrative, it claims to contain 'the secret words which the living Jesus spoke' and sees Jesus' virgin birth and resurrection as naïve misunderstandings. While some sayings may have originated with Jesus, its emphasis on 'secret sayings' probably reflects its influence by second-century Gnostic groups. Its unorthodox teaching led to it, and other similar early writings, being excluded from the canon (the list of accepted Scripture).

How Did We Get the Gospels?

■ After Jesus' resurrection, the message was communicated initially by word-of-mouth (highly accurate in those days). Jesus' style of teaching, using bite-sized chunks and graphic illustrations, made this all the more easy.

■ As the message spread, practical guidance was needed on living out the faith, which led to church leaders writing letters (epistles) *before* the Gospels.

■ They eventually saw that Jesus' story needed writing down so it wouldn't be lost to future generations, leading to the writing of the Gospels.

Can We Trust the Gospels?

While the Gospels acknowledge they have an 'angle' (John 20:30–31), this doesn't mean they aren't reliable. In fact, Luke highlights the historical research behind his Gospel, involving careful investigation of eyewitnesses (Luke 1:1–4). Wherever we can check his facts, even minor geographical and political details, they are accurate. We can therefore be confident that the Gospels' picture of Jesus, while impassioned, is truthful. Where the Gospels sometimes appear contradictory, this probably reflects the fact they are recording similar teaching but from different occasions.

These are written that you may believe that Jesus is the Christ, the Son of God, and that by believing you may have life in his name.

JOHN 20:31

KEY FEATURES OF THE GOSPELS

	MATTHEW	MARK	LUKE	JOHN
AUTHOR	Matthew, one of the twelve disciples	Mark, part of the wider group of disciples; Peter's assistant in Rome	Luke, doctor and Paul's companion; the only Gentile writer in the New Testament	John, one of the twelve disciples
DATE	Mid AD 60s	Late AD 50s	c. AD 59–61	c. AD 85
TARGET AUDIENCE	Jewish Christians	Gentiles (non-Jews)	Gentiles (non-Jews)	Jews and Gentiles
STYLE	Teaching gathered in long blocks	Fast-moving, action-packed, simple language, abrupt ending	Well-researched, accurate detail	Selective; lengthy teaching and discussions
JESUS SEEN AS:	▶ The Messiah who fulfils Israel's hopes and promises ▶ Son of God ▶ Great teacher ▶ A 'greater Moses'	▶ Son of man who suffers for us ▶ Son of God who overcomes evil ▶ Promised Messiah ▶ Teacher (rabbi)	▶ Messiah ▶ Man of the Spirit ▶ David's promised descendant ▶ The man for everyone	▶ Pre-existent 'Word' ▶ God-become-man ▶ The Father's unique Son ▶ Messiah
BIRTH STORIES	Yes	No	Yes	Cosmic beginnings
KEY POINTS	▶ A 'better law' ▶ Denunciation of Pharisees ▶ Kingdom of heaven ▶ Discipleship ▶ Judgment upon Israel	▶ Presence of God's kingdom ▶ Jesus' power ▶ Call to discipleship ▶ Jesus as a different sort of Messiah ▶ The necessity of Jesus' death	▶ Care for the despised and disadvantaged ▶ The Holy Spirit ▶ Healing ▶ Prayer ▶ God's new community	▶ Seven 'signs' and 'discourses' revealing Jesus ▶ 'I am' sayings ▶ Jesus' relationship with God ▶ Contains some of the best-known Bible verses
PARTICULARLY USEFUL FOR:	Understanding how Jesus fits in to the Old Testament story	Starting to learn about Jesus	Seeing Jesus' compassion for the needy	Thinking more reflectively about Jesus

Why Four?

Just like different media sources give different viewpoints about events today, so it is with the Gospels; each has its own viewpoint. Matthew, Mark and Luke have similar content and order and so are called 'synoptic' ('same viewpoint') Gospels; but John writes differently, selecting a few miracles and teachings in order to focus on their significance. In AD 160 Tatian, a theologian and apologist, tried condensing the four accounts into one (called 'Diatesseron') but found it didn't work because of each Gospel's unique perspective. Many early Christian leaders thought four was the ideal number as 'four' symbolized totality or universality in those days.

KEY SAYING

'But the Counsellor, the Holy Spirit, whom the Father will send in my name, will teach you all things and will remind you of everything I have said to you.'

JOHN 14:26

His World

A HYPERMARKET OF LIFE

The world into which Jesus was born was a cultural and religious hypermarket, with no smaller choice of beliefs and lifestyles than today. It was into this setting, with all its alternatives and choices, that Jesus not only came but, stunningly, claimed to be the way, the only way, to find God.

The Roman Empire

Founded in 753 BC by Romulus, Rome initially struggled for many centuries. It became a republic in 509 BC, led by two elected consuls and a senate, and by 272 BC controlled all Italy. It then steadily expanded, defeating Carthage and Corinth in 146 BC and Athens in 86 BC. In the first century BC Julius Caesar conquered Gaul and Britain, while Pompey conquered Syria and Palestine. Octavian became its first emperor in 31 BC, adopting the title Augustus in 27 BC. It was during his reign that Jesus was born.

By New Testament times, Rome's empire was vast, covering Europe, Greece, Asia Minor and North Africa. Its iron hand brought peace and stability; just laws and good administration prevailed; roads linked every city; aqueducts carried water; trade flourished; the denarius became the universal currency. All this produced the *Pax Romana* ('Roman Peace'), which would prove significant in helping the spread of Christianity. Within twenty years of Jesus' death, every major city in the Roman empire would have a church.

SOME GREEK AND ROMAN GODS

Greek name	Roman name	Sphere of influence
Zeus	Jupiter	Chief god
Athena	Minerva	War, wisdom, arts
Apollo	Apollo	Sun, prophecy, poetry, music, medicine
Artemis	Diana	Chastity, hunting, moon
Poseidon	Neptune	Sea, earthquakes, horses
Aphrodite	Venus	Love, beauty
Hermes	Mercury	Travel, commerce, invention, cunning
Ares	Mars	War
Demeter	Ceres	Agriculture, fertility, marriage
Dionysus	Bacchus	Wine, ecstasy

In contrast to Jews, who were monotheists (believing in one God), Greeks and Romans were polytheists, having gods for every aspect of life. Christians antagonized not only Greeks and Romans but also Jews by claiming that Jesus was the one true God.

ITALY
Rome

Carthage

0 — 600 kr
0 — 400

Over 50,000 miles (80,500 km) of paved roads crossed the Roman empire, making travel easier. Together with Greece's gift of a world-language (anyone speaking Greek could be understood almost anywhere), the world couldn't have been better prepared for the first Christians spreading their message.

The Septuagint

As Jews dispersed, most lost the ability to speak Hebrew and so could no longer read God's word. It was therefore translated into Greek, the new world-language, in the third century BC in Alexandria, where many Jews had settled, becoming known as the Septuagint (often abbreviated to the Roman numerals LXX) because seventy scholars translated it. It also put the books of the Bible in their present order.

You have spent enough time in the past doing what pagans choose to do.
1 PETER 4:3

● SEE ALSO
HEROD P. 93
SYNAGOGUE P. 28
ZEALOTS P. 18

The Greek Empire

In 336 BC Alexander the Great conquered and united Greece, formerly weak and divided, expanding it into a great empire covering Asia, Syria, Egypt, Persia and even reaching India. But Alexander's dream wasn't just to create an empire, but a way of life. He wanted to export Greek culture, a process known as Hellenization (from *Hellas* – Greece). Greek art, architecture, customs, sport and ideas all flourished, and Greek became the international language of the day.

The Greeks' focus on humanity clashed with Judaism's God-centred life. Particularly offensive to Jews were theatres, with their often highly erotic plays, and stadiums, where athletes performed naked. This, together with Greek polytheism, made conflict inevitable.

After Alexander's death, his empire was divided, with two opposing empires emerging: the Ptolemaic in North Africa and the Seleucid in western Asia, leaving Judea sandwiched between them. Under the Ptolemies, the Jews experienced tolerance; but when the Seleucids took control, everything changed. Their compulsory Hellenization climaxed in 168 BC with Antiochus IV Epiphanes placing a statue of Zeus in Jerusalem's Temple, leading to the Maccabean revolt. The war dragged on till 128 BC, when Israel secured its freedom and, for a time, became independent.

Greece itself finally gave way to the expanding might of Rome, Athens falling in 86 BC; but the effects of Hellenism have lasted to today.

The Theatre of Dionysus in Athens, where plays were performed in honour of the god Dionysus. Sport also had a religious basis, the Olympic Games being held in honour of Zeus. Religion was central to all Greek life, as the apostle Paul discovered (Acts 17:16–23); but as belief decreased, many turned to philosophy.

The Jewish Diaspora

The Jews had been exiled to Babylon in 586 BC and, while some returned home when the exile ended, many had settled and didn't want to. Others had spread to other nations, reaching Morocco by 200 BC and India by 175 BC. This Diaspora ('Scattering') meant that by Jesus' time Jewish communities could be found across the Mediterranean, and there were more Jews outside Judea than inside it. With no Temple for sacrifices, spirituality focused on studying the Torah (God's Law) and meeting in synagogues. It was to the synagogues that Christians always went to start their preaching (e.g. Acts 13:5, 14; 14:1–3; 17:1–4, 10, 16–17; 18:1–4, 19).

Judea

After brief independence, Israel was invaded by Rome in 63 BC, becoming the Roman province of Judea. Four legions were based there to maintain peace and extract taxes, creating a highly charged political atmosphere. While some appreciated the advantages of Roman rule, the majority resented the presence of godless Gentiles in their land. Following Herod the Great's death in 4 BC, there were many uprisings over the next seventy years as would-be 'messiahs' tried to rescue Israel and re-establish a Jewish kingdom. It's not surprising, therefore, that Pilate, the Roman governor, was anxious on being told that Jesus was claiming to be king of the Jews.

KEY SAYING

'I am the way and the truth and the life. No-one comes to the Father except through me.'

JOHN 14:6

His Land
WHERE PROMISES GET FULFILLED

The land in which Jesus lived was tiny, less than 150 miles (240 km) from north to south and between 25 and 60 miles (40 and 95 km) wide. Yet it was full of history and promises stretching right back to Israel's founder, Abraham (Genesis 12:1–3; 15:12–20; 17:1–8); and Jesus claimed that, through him, those promises were about to be fulfilled. For it was to this tiny geographical area that Jesus came as Israel's promised king, and it was from this tiny geographical area that he would send his message of love and hope into the whole world.

TYPICAL HOMES

Most homes in Jesus' time were made of either stone or mud bricks, generally built around an open courtyard with rooms on three sides. The flat roof, reached by an outside staircase or ladder, was used for everything from drying grain to relaxing in the evening breeze. Animals were brought into homes at night for safety.

Date palms in tropical Jericho, just one of the 2,780 species of plants and trees in Israel. Other common fruits were figs which, like dates, were eaten fresh or dried and made into cakes; grapes, which were dried into raisins or turned into wine; and olives, which were eaten or pressed for oil. Common cereals included wheat and barley for bread (though only the poor used barley) and flax. Many of Jesus' parables were based on scenes from the natural world and daily agricultural life, so were easily accessible to ordinary people.

THE FARMING YEAR

Throughout Bible times, most families made their living from the land. While each family had been given its own plot on entering the Promised Land, which was to be passed on from one generation to another, by New Testament times much of it was owned by foreigners with huge estates. Local farmers rented land from them, often at exorbitant rents. The chart below shows the yearly cycle of farming life.

In areas of poor cultivation, herds of sheep and goats were kept rather than crops grown, though most homes would have an animal or two that shared the house with the family. Each day, besides tending the crops and animals, grain would be ground into flour for baking bread, water collected from nearby wells, and milk obtained and turned into cheese and yoghurt. As still in many parts of the world today, the whole family would have been involved.

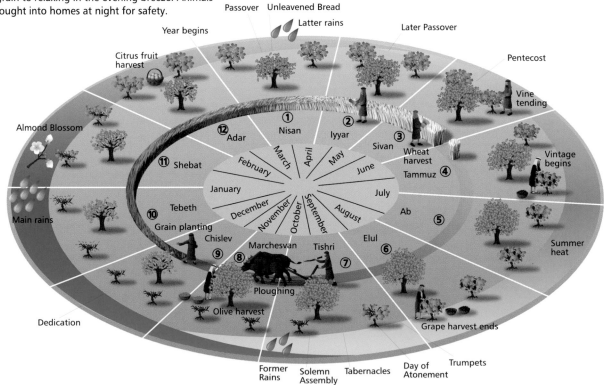

'You are the Son of God; you are the King of Israel.'
JOHN 1:49

SEE ALSO
GALILEE P. 26
HEROD P. 93
ZEALOTS P. 18

Israel's Geography

Israel fell into five clearly definable areas:

1. The coastal plain, comprising sand dunes, forest and swamps in the south but very fertile land in the north. Beyond Mount Carmel there were several natural harbours.

2. The Shephelah, very fertile foothills some 12–15 miles (19–24 km) wide with four valleys running through it as corridors.

3. The Highlands, comprising **(a)** the Judean Hills in the south, home to the capital Jerusalem and **(b)** the Samarian Hills and Galilee to the north, divided by the Valley of Jezreel and the Plain of Megiddo. While the western side of the hills sloped gently to the coast, the eastern side dropped steeply into the Jordan Valley. Its limestone rock was a good source of copper.

The main north–south road crossed the Plain of Megiddo where many battles happened in Old Testament times and where the Bible sees the End Time battle (Armageddon) taking place. The road continued through the fertile lower hills of Galilee, making the area prosperous because of passing trade. Galilee was where Jesus spent most of his life.

4. The Jordan Valley, part of the Great Rift Valley, running from the Sea of Galilee to the Dead Sea, the lowest point on earth, more than 1,300 feet (400 m) below sea level, with its floor a further 1,300 feet down.

5. The Transjordan, a mountainous area, rising from 1,900 feet (580 m) east of Galilee to 6,560 feet (2000 m) south-east of the Dead Sea. It therefore attracted rainfall and provided good pasture for animals; but beyond it lay simply desert.

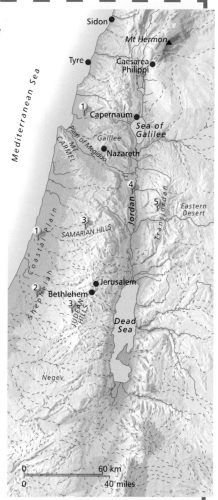

SEA OF GALILEE

'Although God has created seven seas, yet he has chosen this one as his special delight,' the rabbis said about the Sea of Galilee (or the Sea of Tiberias), the focal point of much of Jesus' ministry. The lake had sixty-eight kinds of fish, which generated a lively fishing trade, and several of Jesus' first disciples were fishermen. The lake is 13 miles (20 km) long and 8 miles (13 km) wide at its widest point. From here the Jordan flows down to the Dead Sea, which is 25 per cent salt.

RIVER JORDAN

The Jordan (meaning 'Descender') has lush vegetation lining its banks. Rarely more than 15 yards (13 m) wide, it is a slow and meandering river, covering 200 miles (325 km), twice the direct distance. From its northern beginnings to the Dead Sea in the south the river drops 2,380 feet (725 m). Being below sea level, it couldn't be used for irrigation like the Nile in Egypt or the Tigris and Euphrates in Persia, leaving Israel completely dependent on rainfall. It was, as Moses described it, 'a land of mountains and valleys that drinks rain from heaven' (Deuteronomy 11:11).

The prevailing winds from the Mediterranean dropped their moisture over the central Highlands, leaving little for land in their shadow. The rains came at three points in the year (October, January and April), with no rain at all between mid May and mid October, so reliable water supplies through wells and cisterns (underground storage tanks) were very important.

A cross-section of the land. Jerusalem, being so high, could get chilly in winter (5–10 degrees Celsius), but south of the Dead Sea it could easily reach 50 degrees Celsius in summer. Galilee, Jesus' home, varied between 10 and 35 degrees Celsius.

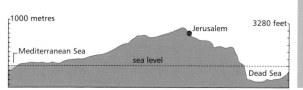

KEY SAYING

'Blessed are the meek, for they will inherit the earth.'
MATTHEW 5:5

His Nation

A CHOSEN PEOPLE

Jesus was born a Jew, part of God's chosen people to whom he had given many promises. But those promises seemed slow in coming; and even though they had returned from exile centuries earlier, many still felt in exile, spiritually speaking. Not only had the prophets' vision of new beginnings not happened, but Israel was now subject to Rome. Some responded by co-operating, some by fighting, some by retreating, but most by getting on with life. It was into this mixture of hopes and fears that Jesus came to kick-start God's ancient promises.

Languages

There were four main languages in Palestine in Jesus' day. **Hebrew** was the ancient language of the Jews and their Scriptures, but was now generally confined to religious ceremonies and was the preserve of scholars and the educated. Most ordinary people spoke **Aramaic**, which had become the dominant language of the Middle East. Various accents existed, which is why Peter, with his northern accent, was recognized at an inconvenient moment (Matthew 26:73). **Greek** had been common since Alexander the Great's conquest of Palestine in 332 BC. As the official language of the eastern Roman empire, it was the language of diplomacy and commerce, so even fishermen like Peter probably spoke Greek for trading their fish. **Latin** was less important, probably confined to Romans speaking among themselves.

Jesus spoke Aramaic (Mark 5:41; 7:34; 15:34), Greek (Mark 7:26; John 7:35; 12:20–21) and at least enough Hebrew to read God's word (Luke 4:16–20). When he was crucified, the charge against him was written in Aramaic, Latin and Greek (John 19:19–20) so everyone could understand.

PALESTINE IN JESUS' TIME

After Herod the Great's death in 4 BC, Rome divided his kingdom between his three sons; but the ineffective Archelaus was replaced by a Roman governor, Pilate, who ruled from AD 26 to 36 and who was responsible for having Jesus crucified (Matthew 27:11–26).

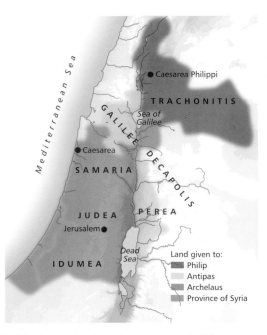

Political Atmosphere

While Israel had experienced independence after the Maccabean revolt in the second century BC, it wasn't long before it was conquered once again, this time by Rome in 63 BC. Rome's presence produced a highly charged political atmosphere. While some appreciated the advantages of Roman rule – things like peace and stability – the majority resented the presence of godless Gentiles (non-Jews). Some, like the Essenes, retreated into the desert, devoting themselves to prayer; others, like the Zealots, took every opportunity to oppose Rome and, following Herod's death, there were many messianic uprisings over the next seventy years.

Jerusalem

Seen here is a model of first-century Jerusalem, from the south-west. The city of Jerusalem was dominated by the Temple, which covered 35 acres, about one-fifth of the city. Above it towered the Fortress of Antonia (named in honour of Mark Anthony), housing the Roman garrison of 600 soldiers. To its west were the homes of the wealthy and Herod's palace, while below it the homes of the poor huddled together in narrow streets. Jerusalem's population was around 30,000 in Jesus' time, though this swelled to five times that number at festivals.

The LORD your God has chosen you out of all the peoples on the face of the earth to be his people, his treasured possession.

DEUTERONOMY 7:6

● SEE ALSO
CLEANSING OF TEMPLE P. 33
HIS PEOPLE PP. 18–19
MACCABEAN REVOLT P. 16

The Temple

The Temple stood at the heart of a series of courtyards:

1 The Court of the Gentiles, the nearest Gentiles could go to pray. Columns 50 feet (15 m) high divided the surrounding portico into three aisles, each 30 feet (9 m) wide. This area had become a market for animal-sellers and money-changers, which angered Jesus since it hindered Gentiles from praying.

2 The Court of the Women, with four huge candelabra, the furthest that Jewish women and children could go.

3 The Court of Israel, where Jewish men brought their animals for sacrifice.

4 The Court of the Priests, where the sacrifices were offered by priests.

5 The Sanctuary, containing the Holy of Holies, symbolizing God's presence.

A sign in Greek prohibiting non-Jews from entering the inner courts. It says: 'No outsider shall enter the enclosure around the sanctuary. Whoever is caught doing so will have himself to blame for his death.'

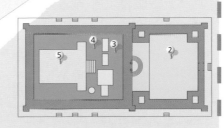

A silver denarius from the reign of Tiberius (AD 14–37). The denarius, the daily wage for a labourer, was the most common coin of the time. It was this coin that Jesus used when he told opponents trying to trick him to 'Give to Caesar what is Caesar's and to God what is God's' (Mark 12:17). Herod Antipas, the ruler of Galilee, avoided putting images on his coins, as the deified emperor's image was offensive to Jews.

Attitudes to the Temple

While the Temple was the central symbol of Israel's life, Herod's rebuilding of it – an attempt to legitimize his kingship since he was Idumean not Jewish – met with mixed reactions. While the priestly aristocracy approved of it, since their monopoly of the sacrificial system gave them power, many disapproved:

■ **The Essenes** saw the Temple as the power base of the ruling elite, ritually impure because God's Law wasn't interpreted properly there, and flawed because it didn't match Ezekiel's vision of the new Temple (Ezekiel 40–48).

■ **The Pharisees** believed that the blessing of visiting the Temple could just as equally be gained by studying the Torah, so the Temple's existence wasn't crucial for them.

■ **The common people** saw the Temple as a symbol of all that oppressed them, especially the corrupt aristocracy.

Jesus too was opposed to the Temple, but for completely different reasons: he simply believed it had served its purpose and therefore its time had come. It symbolized everything that was wrong with Israel and would therefore be destroyed (Mark 13:1–2; 14:58). He saw himself as the new temple, the 'place' where sin could be forgiven.

KEY SAYING

'O Jerusalem... how often I have longed to gather your children together, as a hen gathers her chicks under her wings, but you were not willing!'

LUKE 13:34

His People

FIRST-CENTURY JUDAISM

Describing what first-century Jews thought isn't easy, for Judaism was a complex phenomenon, with huge social, spiritual and political divisions that produced many cross-currents and widely different expectations. Somehow, Jesus managed to upset almost everyone, challenging hopes and vested interests. Yet it was in the history of this people that his own roots firmly lay.

Key Groupings

While most people didn't belong to any particular grouping, there were four major ones in Jesus' time:

■ **The Pharisees** ('separated ones' or 'specifiers') were the largest group, numbering around 6,000 and strongest in Galilee where Jesus lived. Being a Pharisee wasn't a job (most were middle-class merchants) but a lifestyle, involving rigorous application of God's word to every aspect of life. Their influence was significant and their vision widely accepted (even if ordinary people felt they couldn't live up to it). While often parodied as hypocrites concerned only with externals, their stress on purity and obedience to God's Law wasn't an end in itself but, in their eyes, crucial to maintaining Israel's identity, believing this alone could pave the way for God liberating his people. They therefore put great stress on identity markers, such as circumcision, tithing, Sabbath and ritual cleanliness.

■ **The Sadducees**, while fewer in number, were more influential, being the 'establishment' figures of the day. Descended from Zadok, King Solomon's high priest, they controlled the Temple, chose the high priest and dominated the Sanhedrin, the Jewish ruling council. More conservative than the Pharisees, they accepted only Moses' writings (the Bible's first five books), rejecting any doctrines that weren't found there (like resurrection) as well as the Pharisees' oral traditions.

■ **The Essenes** followed 'a severer discipline' (Josephus), having broken away 200 years earlier from the Temple authorities whom they saw as lax. While some lived among ordinary people, most joined alternative communities, like that at Qumran, where they lived out their ideals in an ascetic lifestyle of brotherly love and strict adherence to the Jewish Law as they waited for God to bring the end of the age.

■ **The Zealots**, unlike the Essenes, weren't prepared to wait for God; they wanted to help him out. Founded by Judas the Galilean in AD 6, these guerrilla fighters believed that Israel had no king but God alone and so opposed Rome. Preferring daggers to prayer, they fought to bring God's kingdom and led several revolts, one of which led to Jerusalem's destruction in AD 70.

> ### JOSEPHUS SAID...
> 'Sadducees persuade only the well-to-do and have no popular following. But the Pharisees have the masses as allies.' (*Antiquities*, 12.297–298)

Qumran, an Essene community near the Dead Sea. Its ruins include a scriptorium, where the Dead Sea Scrolls were probably written, and several baptismal cisterns for ritual washings.

A Jewish prayer-shawl with its distinctive blue stripes and tassels. God had told the Jews to wear tassels to remember they were his people (Numbers 15:38–39), but by Jesus' time, Pharisees wore extra-long tassels as an ostentatious mark of piety, which Jesus rebuked (Matthew 23:5).

He came to his own country, but his own people did not receive him.
JOHN 1:11

● SEE ALSO
HIS LAND PP. 14–15
HIS NATION PP. 16–17
HIS OPPONENTS PP. 92–93

Jesus' Genealogy

While first-century hopes were very mixed, all were rooted in Israel's history, which is why Matthew and Luke record Jesus' genealogy, to underline that his coming was part of God's ongoing plan through his people. Comparison of those genealogies (Matthew 1:1–17; Luke 3:23–38) reveals some differences – not mistakes or contradictions, but rather two different genealogical lines: Matthew follows the line of Joseph (Jesus' legal father) and Luke the line of Mary (Jesus' blood mother), both of whom were descended from Israel's great King David. Matthew's genealogy begins with Abraham, the founder of the Jewish faith, to show Jesus has the right to fulfil God's promises to him; but Luke's goes right back to Adam, underlining that Jesus came not just for Jews, but for everyone.

A Jewish family praying together at the start of a Sabbath meal.

New Identity

Although the Jewish sense of family identity was strong, Jesus sometimes cut across it. He challenged one man to abandon his wealth, held in the form of land (Luke 18:18–30), for the land of Israel had now been superseded in importance in God's plan. He told another to abandon his duty of burying his father and follow him, leaving the dead to bury their dead (Luke 9:59–60), shocking in a culture in which burying your father took priority even over prayer. Jesus did this because, although he was rooted in the history of God's people, he was convinced that what God was doing through him was building a brand new family, a brand new nation – nothing less than a reconstituted people of God.

Clothing

Most people wore open-neck tunics, knee-length for men, full-length for women, tied at the sides and fastened with a belt, and an outer cloak. All but the poor wore sandals and head-coverings. Clothes were made from wool or linen, but linen or silk for the rich. Dyes were made from plants, animals and minerals; black, blue, red, yellow and green were all popular colours. Purple, expensive to produce, was the preserve of the wealthy. Scientific analysis of clothing fragments from the Bar Kokhba war (AD 132–135) revealed that just three basic dyes (saffron yellow, indigo blue and alazarin red) were used to produce thirty-four different colours of thread.

Masada, Herod the Great's former palace, rising 1,500 feet (460 m) above the Dead Sea. Over 900 Zealots made a last-ditch stand against Rome here after Jerusalem's destruction in AD 70, holding out for three years. When the Romans built an enormous siege-ramp, it became clear their fight was hopeless and they took their own lives, each man killing his own family and then one another, leaving the final man to commit suicide.

KEY SAYING

'I have compassion for these people.'
MARK 8:2

His Coming
THE GOD WHO BREAKS IN

For hundreds of years Israel's prophets had spoken of Messiah's coming; but with the passing of time, and now the brutal presence of Rome, that sometimes seemed hard to believe. But in a world that God had been carefully preparing, the moment had now come. God was about to break into the human dimension as never before, this time not sending a prophet, but coming himself.

A Surprise Announcement

People in the first century weren't naïve: they knew as well as us how pregnancy happened. That's why, when God sent the angel Gabriel to tell Mary she would become pregnant and give birth to God's Son (what Christians call 'the annunciation'), she understandably replied, 'How will this be... since I am a virgin?' (Luke 1:34). It's also why Joseph, her fiancé, decided not to proceed with marriage, though he still loved Mary enough not to dishonour her (Matthew 1:18–19). Only God's miraculous revelation through an angel visiting him in a dream convinced him Mary was telling the truth: her child had indeed been conceived miraculously by God's Spirit and not by any man, and this child was the long-awaited Saviour (Matthew 1:20–21).

The Virgin Birth

While some have dismissed the virgin birth as impossible, or merely a literary device for saying that Jesus was somehow 'special', it is central to traditional Christian understanding of who Jesus is and why he came. With the virgin birth, God was starting humanity all over again through Jesus: a brand new, perfect human being, created in Mary's womb by God's Spirit, which meant he didn't inherit Adam and Eve's sin like everyone else. The Bible says it is this 'sinlessness' which made it possible for Jesus to die for us, paying the price not of his own sin (for he had none), but ours. Remove *his* virgin birth and you remove *our* forgiveness.

The belief that Mary remained a virgin throughout life ('perpetual virginity') arose later in church history, though this isn't claimed in the New Testament itself which simply notes that Joseph 'had no union with her until she gave birth to a son' (Matthew 1:25). Matthew also records that Jesus had brothers and sisters (Matthew 12:46; 13:55–56), though Catholic scholars interpret these as cousins.

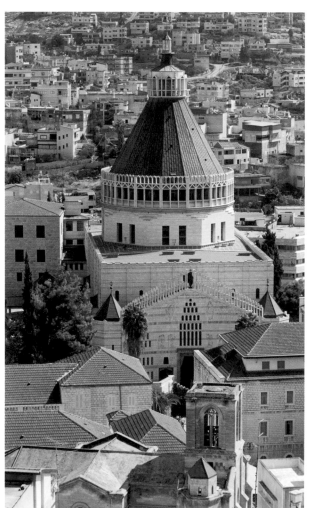

Nazareth's Church of the Annunciation, the traditional site of Mary's encounter with the angel. Although the Roman Catholic basilica dates only from the 1960s, Christians have worshipped at this site from earliest times. An alternative site is marked by the Greek Orthodox church built over the town's water source.

Mary's Magnificat

When Mary discovered she was indeed pregnant, she burst into singing (Luke 1:46–55), a song Christians call the 'Magnificat' from its opening word in Latin and which is still used by many in worship. From the fourth century, Mary gradually acquired a more central place in many Christians' thinking, largely through a desire to maintain Jesus' true humanity, becoming known as 'the Mother of God'. While some theologians were unhappy with this, the trend continued, and Mary is still important to many Christians today.

When the right time came, God sent his Son...
GALATIANS 4:4

● SEE ALSO
HIS FAMILY PP. 26–27
INCARNATION P. 24
NAZARETH P. 27

Dreams

While often found in the Bible as a means of God communicating with people, in the Gospels dreams are confined to Matthew and all focus on Jesus, reflecting God's watchful care over his life from beginning to end. Through dreams:

■ Mary's conception is explained to Joseph (1:20)

■ The wise men are warned not to return to Herod (2:12)

■ Joseph is told to flee to Egypt (2:13)

■ Joseph is warned against returning to Judea (2:22)

■ Pilate's wife is troubled about Jesus (27:19)

While dreams are far more common in the Old Testament than in the New, Peter reminded his hearers at Pentecost that 'In the last days, God says, I will pour out my Spirit on all people. Your sons and daughters will prophesy, your young men will see visions, your old men will dream dreams' (Acts 2:17), suggesting God can still use dreams to speak to people.

ANGELS

While generally portrayed in art as having long robes and wings, angels in the Bible are much more 'human', at times mistaken for people, even though they are spirit-beings. 'Angel' means 'messenger', for their role was to bring God's message, as they did to Mary and Joseph. Angels are mentioned over 180 times in the New Testament, not only bringing God's message, but also his help, protection, direction and judgment.

In this stained glass window, the angel brings news to Mary.

The early church saw the virgin birth as fulfilling Isaiah's prophecy given over 700 years earlier: 'The virgin will be with child and will give birth to a son, and they will call him Immanuel – which means, "God with us"' (Isaiah 7:14; Matthew 1:23).

Marriage

In New Testament times, marriage was a two-stage event. It began with betrothal (engagement), as binding as marriage and requiring divorce to end it (see Matthew 1:18–19). One year later, the marriage took place, often with little notice, and the groom took his bride home. It was during this year that Joseph discovered Mary was pregnant. She was probably about fourteen years old.

THE MEANING OF 'JESUS'

'Jesus' was the Greek form of the Old Testament name 'Joshua', meaning 'the LORD saves'. However, Jesus' salvation would have a twist to it: whereas Jews believed it was *others* who needed saving, the angel said that 'he will save *his* people from *their* sins' (Matthew 1:21). In other words, salvation needed to begin with them – never an easy message to bring to an oppressed people who think their problems are everybody else's fault. This message would bring Jesus into constant conflict with religious leaders.

KEY SAYING

'For God so loved the world that he gave his one and only Son, that whoever believes in him shall not perish but have eternal life.'
JOHN 3:16

His Birth
THE CHRISTMAS STORY

The Christmas story is one of the best-known stories in the world, re-enacted annually in countless nativity plays. Yet its meaning passes by so many people, reduced to some vague message about family life or peace on earth. The truth of the story is mind-blowing, however: for the baby in the manger was the long-awaited Saviour – no one less than God himself.

When Was Jesus Born?

Since we date everything before Christ (BC) or after Christ (AD = *Anno Domini*, 'in the year of our Lord'), we might have expected Jesus to be born in '0' or 'AD 1', but he wasn't. It was probably in 5 BC, a date that fits both the first census of Quirinius, the Roman governor of the province of Syria, and the appearance of a tailed comet, confirmed by ancient Chinese records and modern astronomy. Our modern calendar was simply calculated incorrectly by the monk Dionysius in AD 525.

But not only is the year wrong, so is the date! Jesus was probably born in April, during lambing season, when shepherds would have been 'keeping watch over their flocks at night' (Luke 2:8). This also fits the Chinese records which say the comet appeared between 9 March and 6 April. The date 25 December only became fixed in the Western church in the fourth century to replace the pagan festival of Sol Invictus (the Invincible Sun). The Eastern Orthodox Church, following the Gregorian calendar, celebrates Christmas on 7 January however.

THE SHEPHERDS

After Jesus' birth an angel directed shepherds to visit the newborn saviour (Luke 2:8–20). Shepherds were poor and, according to rabbinic tradition, 'unclean', which is why they needed a sign, to assure them they would be welcome. Yet these were the first to hear of the newborn saviour's arrival, an early indication that Jesus would welcome everyone. The shepherds' place (and what they represent) is immortalized in Western art, with nativity scenes frequently including them.

The Adoration of the Shepherds by Esteban Murillo.

No Room at the Inn?

Traditional nativity plays locate Jesus' birth in a stable 'because there was no room for them in the inn' (Luke 2:7), but the word 'inn' really means 'guest room' (as in Luke 22:11); when Luke means 'inn' he uses a different Greek word (as in Luke 10:34). However, most translations retain 'inn' simply because it is so ingrained in tradition.

While homes generally had a 'guest room', the return of the extended family for the census probably meant the family home was packed when Joseph and Mary arrived, the usual three-day journey perhaps extended by her condition. An adjacent cave, often used for storage and animals, would therefore have provided a warm, private place for the birth.

'She wrapped him in cloths and placed him in a manger' (Luke 2:7). A manger (feeding trough), generally made of stone, as shown here, would have made an excellent crib for Jesus once lined with straw.

While Eastern Christianity sees Mary alone when giving birth (reflected in the altar being out of sight of worshippers), Middle Eastern custom and hospitality almost certainly meant the village midwife and female family members would have helped Mary. Jesus would have been rubbed with salt to cleanse and toughen his skin, something still practised in parts of the Middle East, and strips of cloth wrapped around him in the belief that this helped the bones grow straight and strong.

The time came for the baby to be born, and she gave birth to her firstborn, a son.
LUKE 2:6–7

● SEE ALSO
ANGELS P. 21
HIS SILENT YEARS PP. 26–27
INCARNATION P.24

WHY BETHLEHEM?

Although his parents lived in Nazareth, Jesus was born in Bethlehem, 6 miles (10 km) south of Jerusalem. The human reason for this was a census, important for assessing taxes, for which everyone had to return to their native home (Luke 2:1–4). But God was also at work; for Bethlehem, Micah had prophesied 700 years earlier, was where Messiah would be born (Micah 5:2–4; John 7:41–42). While men usually represented their families in legal matters, the province of Syria also taxed women, which may explain why Mary accompanied him. But equally, Joseph may have taken her out of kindness, rather than leaving her in Nazareth where rumours about her pregnancy were probably still rife.

Visitors from the East

While traditional nativity plays portray Jesus' final visitors as kings, they were in fact Arabian 'magi'. Babylon and Persia were great centres of astronomy and astrology, where magi were a mixture of priests, astronomers and royal advisers, and where they helped develop Zoroastrianism. In Old Testament times Daniel, exiled to Babylon (Daniel 1:1–7), had been appointed chief of the magi by Nebuchadnezzar (Daniel 2:48), so it may have been from him that they learned of God's coming saviour.

Contrary to tradition, we have no idea how many magi came (the traditional number three is based solely on the number of gifts) nor when they came, though it was probably several weeks, if not months, later. Two main reasons support this: first, when they arrived, the family was now in 'the house', not the stable (Matthew 2:11), into which they had presumably moved after the extended family had departed; second, Herod's massacre of infant boys up to two years old (Matthew 2:16–18) suggests that, even allowing for Herod wanting a large margin of error, quite a period of time had elapsed.

The Adoration of the Kings, by Johann Friedrich Overbeck, 1813.

CIRCUMCISION

At eight days old, Jesus was named and circumcised (Luke 2:21), using traditional implements like these. Circumcision went back to Abraham and was a sign of belonging to God's covenant people (Genesis 17:9–14). Five weeks later, his parents took him to Jerusalem's Temple where they dedicated him to God and where Simeon and Anna prophesied over him (Luke 2:22–38).

KEY SAYING

'I have come in my Father's name.'

JOHN 5:43

His Origins
THE ETERNAL CHRIST

Unlike everyone who has ever lived, the beginning of Jesus' life was not the beginning of him; he had existed from the beginning of everything. The staggering message of Christianity is that Jesus, the eternal Son of God, took human form and came among us. It is a claim that sounds as foolish or blasphemous today as it did in New Testament times (see 1 Corinthians 1:18–25); but remove this aspect of who Jesus was, and you remove the very essence and uniqueness of Christianity.

Jesus' Humanity

While the Bible claims Jesus was fully God, it also shows he was fully human, not some hybrid creation or Superman-like figure. The Bible demonstrates Jesus' humanness in things like:

■ He experienced normal human development (Luke 2:40, 52)

■ He got tired (e.g. Luke 8:23; John 4:6)

■ He experienced hunger and thirst (e.g. Matthew 4:2; John 19:28)

■ He bled and died (John 19:32–34)

Some early Christians, influenced by Gnostic cults, struggled to believe that Jesus was fully human, and John's stress on Jesus becoming 'flesh' ('real flesh and blood', as we might say) may have been to answer this.

The Incarnation

At the heart of Christianity lies 'the incarnation' (from the Latin *in carne*, meaning 'in the flesh'). This is the belief that Jesus was not a prophet or holy man, but none less than God himself in human flesh. Jesus did this, not by wearing some human cloak and seeming to be human, nor by becoming some half-man, half-god, but by emptying himself of his God-ness and taking on humanity. He was God-become-man, the same eternal being that he had always been, but now in a different form of existence, just like a butterfly is exactly the same being as the caterpillar it came from before its metamorphosis. Look at Jesus, the New Testament says, and you are looking at God himself.

The Miraculous Transformation

The early church never ceased to be amazed at the miraculous transformation that the Son of God experienced in the incarnation. Several key New Testament passages sum this up:

	THE ETERNAL JESUS	THE HUMAN JESUS
JOHN	In the beginning was the Word, and the Word was with God, and the Word was God. He was with God in the beginning (John 1:1–2)	The Word became flesh and made his dwelling among us (John 1:14).
PAUL	Who, being in very nature God, did not consider equality with God something to be grasped… (Philippians 2:6).	… but made himself nothing, taking the very nature of a servant, being made in human likeness (Philippians 2:6–7).
WRITER OF HEBREWS	The Son is the radiance of God's glory and the exact representation of his being, sustaining all things by his powerful word (Hebrews 1:3).	Because God's children are human beings – made of flesh and blood – Jesus also became flesh and blood by being born in human form (Hebrews 2:14, NLT).

In the beginning was the Word, and the Word was with God, and the Word was God... The Word became flesh and made his dwelling among us.
JOHN 1:1, 14

● SEE ALSO
HIS RELATIONSHIP TO GOD PP. 80–81
JESUS' GENEALOGY P. 19
VIRGIN BIRTH P. 20

JESUS, GOD'S GLORY

'*The Word became flesh and made his dwelling [literally, "tabernacled"] among us*' (John 1:14). The tabernacle was the special tent used during Israel's wilderness journey that symbolized God's glorious presence in their midst; but packed away for travel, it looked nothing special, covered as it was with animal skins. Likewise, John says, on the outside Jesus looked nothing special (Isaiah 53:2); but underneath this outward appearance there was the very glory of God.

Did Jesus Know He Was God?

If Jesus had truly become human, did he know he was God? Or did it mean there were now some things he couldn't know, like the date of his return, for example (Matthew 24:36), and whether he was God? There are certainly clear indications he understood his 'specialness'; for example, forgiving people (something only God could do); letting people call him Lord and even God; seeing himself as 'I am' (God's name in the Old Testament), to mention just a few. Certainly by the age of twelve he was aware of a special relationship with God, telling his worried parents, who thought they had lost him, 'Didn't you know I had to be in my Father's house?' (Luke 2:49). No Jew would ever dare to claim that God was his personal Father (he was just the Father of Israel), and yet Jesus did. Clearly he understood *something* of his uniqueness.

And what about his mother, Mary? After all, she knew at least something of who he was from the angel (Luke 1:31–33, 35). It seems highly unlikely she wouldn't have shared such news with her son as he grew up.

THE MYSTERY OF THE TRINITY

How can God be one (an Old Testament fundamental, e.g. Deuteronomy 6:4), yet also be three? This mystery of 'the Trinity' – that the Father, Son and Holy Spirit are all equally and fully God, yet are not three but one – is never set out formally in the New Testament; yet it was the conclusion church leaders reached on the basis of the evidence before them. The first recorded use of the word 'Trinity' (*Trinitas* in Latin) occurs around AD 180, but a final agreed doctrine wasn't formulated until AD 325 at the Council of Nicea.

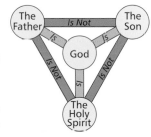

This illustration, originally with Latin text, is known as 'The Shield of the Trinity' or 'The Shield of Faith' and dates from the twelfth century AD. In medieval England and France it was thought of as God's coat of arms. Many other illustrations have been suggested over the centuries, including the modern one of a cube which, while having three equal dimensions, makes only one cube. Take away any dimension and you have taken away the cube.

KEY SAYING

'*Anyone who has seen me has seen the Father.*'
JOHN 14:9

His Silent Years

LIFE IN THE SHADOWS

Of the first thirty years of Jesus' life, we know almost nothing. Matthew and Luke narrate the circumstances of his birth; John peeks behind the scenes to see his cosmic beginnings; Mark launches straight in to his ministry; but none of them tell us anything about what happened in the silent years in Nazareth. Yet these were years when God's Son was being quietly prepared for his lifetime's work.

What Happened to Joseph?

The last we ever hear of Joseph is during his visit to Jerusalem when Jesus was twelve. So what happened to him? The most likely explanation is that he died when Jesus was a teenager. This might explain why Jesus, as eldest son, stayed home until he was thirty, since he would have had to take responsibility for the family as the new head of household, only leaving to begin his ministry when his siblings (Matthew 12:47; 13:55) were old enough to carry responsibility themselves.

From Bethlehem to Nazareth

The first months of Jesus' life were a portent of the trouble ahead. Warned by an angel of Herod's infanticide, Joseph fled with Mary and Jesus to Egypt for safety (Matthew 2:13–15), where there had been Jewish settlements since some had fled there at the time of exile in 586 BC. Here they remained until Herod's death in 4 BC, and Matthew sees a parallel between what happened to Jesus and what happened to Israel when it too spent time in Egypt before returning to the Promised Land (2:17–18). After Herod's death, an angel told Joseph it was safe to go back. However, Herod's replacement in Judea and Samaria was Archelaus, a cruel ruler; so, having been warned in a dream, Joseph took his family back to Nazareth in Galilee (Matthew 2:19–23).

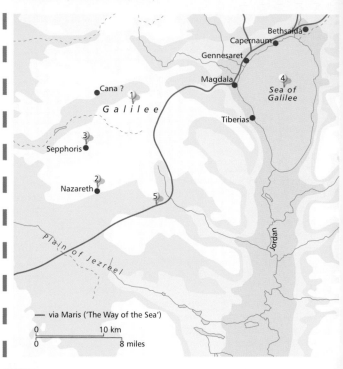

The fertile Plain of Jezreel in southern Galilee is today one of the most productive areas of Israel.

1. GALILEE

Galilee was divided into two: Upper Galilee in the north, where the hills rose to over 3,000 feet (1,000 m), and Lower Galilee in the south, where the hills were lower. Under Herod the Great and Herod Antipas, Galilee became prosperous, exporting wheat, olives, wine and fish. The mainly Jewish population of around 250,000 was primarily lower class, but with a larger than usual middle class. Attitudes were generally conservative, hence the many synagogues, and the Pharisees were well supported. With its strong regional accent (Matthew

And Jesus grew in wisdom and stature, and in favour with God and men.

LUKE 2:52

● SEE ALSO
HIS FAITH PP. 28–29
HIS LAND PP. 14–15
HIS NATION PP. 16–17

26:73), Galilee was seen as rather backward by Jerusalem.

2. NAZARETH

Nazareth, in Lower Galilee, was a small village of between 100 and 200 people. Not mentioned in the Old Testament, it wasn't really settled until the second century BC, when Maccabean nationalists imported settlers from Judea into 'Galilee of the Gentiles' (Isaiah 9:1); so it may still have been very nationalistic. It was here that Jesus spent most of his life.

3. SEPPHORIS

Sepphoris, Galilee's capital, was just 4 miles (6.5 km) north of Nazareth. Destroyed by the Romans in 4 BC following a riot triggered by Herod the Great's death, Herod Antipas immediately began rebuilding it in splendid style, Josephus describing it as 'the ornament of all Galilee' (*Antiquities*, 18:7). Major building works were happening there throughout Jesus' life, so since his father was in the building trade, they may have been involved in projects there.

4. SEA OF GALILEE

Also called the Sea of Gennesaret and the Sea of Tiberias, this lake was the source of a thriving fishing industry. After Jesus' rejection by Nazareth, he made the towns around its shore the base for his ministry.

5. THE VIA MARIS

This was a major north–south trade route running through the Plain of Jezreel and the heart of Galilee. From the nearby hills Jesus could have seen the whole world passing by.

BAR MITZVAH

At the age of thirteen, Jesus would have marked reaching adulthood in his Bar Mitzvah ('Son of the Commandment') ceremony, just like Jewish boys today. In the preceding months, the rabbi (religious teacher) would have trained him to read passages from God's word in Hebrew, which would be read aloud at the ceremony in the synagogue. He was now considered old enough to understand and obey the Law.

The ruins of Sepphoris. The Roman theatre, seating 4,000, dates from the second century AD.

Education
. . . .

Much of Jesus' education would have happened at home; but from the age of six he probably received some teaching in the synagogue, especially in history, religion and reading God's word. While girls learned practical skills from their mother, such as spinning, weaving and cooking, boys learned their father's trade. Traditionally people think of Joseph and Jesus as carpenters; however, the word Mark used (Mark 6:3) means 'general builder', which may explain why Jesus used building illustrations in his teaching.

Lost and Found
. . . .

Three times a year Jewish men had to attend the Temple in Jerusalem for the Festivals of Passover, Pentecost and Tabernacles. Luke describes an occasion when Joseph took his family there for Passover when Jesus was twelve. Even by this age, Jesus was showing considerable knowledge of God's word, listening to rabbis and questioning them, and drawing admiration for his understanding and answers (Luke 2:46–47). He became so engrossed in discussion that he forgot to leave; and it was only later that his parents, each perhaps thinking he was with the other among the great crowds, discovered he was missing. Another frantic day followed as they journeyed back, and it was only on the third day they found him. Any parent who has temporarily lost a child knows the panic that must have filled their hearts; yet Jesus was surprised they didn't know that he had to be 'in my Father's house' (Luke 2:49), showing an already deep awareness of a special relationship with God.

KEY SAYING

'Didn't you know I had to be in my Father's house?'

LUKE 2:49

His Faith
FOLLOWING THE ONE GOD

Jesus was born a Jew, lived a Jew, died a Jew; so while his message is universal, it is best understood against his Jewish background. However, Jesus didn't handle the Judaism of his day with kid gloves; indeed, he said it was worn out, no longer fit for purpose, and in desperate need of transformation – by him. And yet that transformation was itself the ultimate completion of the story begun in the Old Testament.

Fundamental Jewish Beliefs

■ **God:** There is only one God and therefore he alone should be worshipped (Deuteronomy 6:4–5). Although transcendent, he can be known and involves himself in human lives and history.

Jesus too believed in this one God (making his claims to divinity all the more remarkable), seeing himself as God's ultimate involvement with people.

■ **God's people:** Israel was God's chosen people, called to show what knowing and trusting God looked like, called to be a light to others so they too could know this God.

Jesus said Israel had become introverted, concerned only with protecting its own status and failing in the call to take God's light to others. Jesus would therefore become the beginning of 'new Israel', a new people of God.

■ **God's law:** God's Law (or 'Torah', meaning guidance, instruction), summed up in the Ten Commandments (Exodus 20:1–17), was his manual for good relationships with him and one another and was seen as one of God's chief gifts to Israel.

Jesus accepted the abiding nature and authority of this Law, saying he had come to 'fulfil' it (Matthew 5:17–18), which he did through obeying its commands and bringing about its promises. However, he also radically reinterpreted it, getting back to the very heart of it: a living relationship between God and his people for their good.

PRAYER

Jews praying at the Western (or Wailing) Wall in Jerusalem. In Jesus' time Jews prayed twice a day, at morning and evening sacrifices (9 a.m. and 3 p.m.), though some prayed three times daily, praying also at midday. Prayer began with the *Shema*, Israel's declaration of faith (Deuteronomy 6:4–5), followed by eighteen prayers called *Tefillah* ('Prayer') or *Amidah* ('Standing', because they prayed standing), which were prayed out loud. These prayers are still used today.

THE SYNAGOGUE

The synagogue (Greek for 'gathering') originated during Israel's exile in Babylon. With the Jerusalem Temple destroyed, Jews had to develop a new focus for worship and preserving their beliefs, and synagogues (originally open-air gatherings, Psalm 137:1–3) met that need. Scriptures were read, a sermon preached and prayers said. Synagogues (like this one in the reconstructed 'Nazareth Village') had seating all around and a single door that often faced Jerusalem. It was here that Jesus read a passage from the scroll of Isaiah that prophesied his liberating ministry. His hearers' initial welcome quickly turned to hostility and they tried to kill him (Luke 4:16–30).

*Hear, O Israel: The L*ORD* our God, the L*ORD* is one. Love the L*ORD* your God with all your heart and with all your soul and with all your strength.*

DEUTERONOMY 6:4–5

● SEE ALSO
HIS ATTITUDES TO RELIGION PP. 74–75
SABBATH P. 29
TEMPLE P. 17

Festivals

Pictured is a Jewish family celebrating Passover, one of the three great annual Jewish festivals that Jesus would have celebrated:

■ **Passover**, or Feast of Unleavened Bread, celebrated at full moon in the Jewish month of Nisan (March/April), recalled God's freeing of Israel from slavery in Egypt by 'passing over' their homes and sparing their firstborn (Exodus 12). The story is relived over a special meal, with various foods representing different aspects of the story.

■ **Pentecost**, or Feast of Harvest or Feast of Weeks, celebrated the main wheat harvest in May/June and came seven weeks (Pentecost means 'fiftieth day') after cutting the first grain and presenting the first sheaf to God. In the ceremony, two loaves made from the new flour were offered to God.

■ **Tabernacles**, or Feast of Ingathering, celebrated both the fruit harvest in September/October and Israel's living in 'tabernacles' (tents) on the journey from Egypt to the Promised Land. In New Testament times this was a very popular festival and one of the best attended.

John's Gospel shows Jesus participating in these festivals, going up to Jerusalem as the Law required (Deuteronomy 16:16).

A menorah, a traditional symbol of Israel. Its six branches symbolize the world's creation in six days and the central branch represents the Sabbath. Four giant candelabra stood in the Court of the Women in the Jerusalem Temple, the focus of Israel's faith in Jesus' day; but Jesus would challenge the way the Temple now simply represented corrupted religion.

Other Religious Practices

Some of the other religious practices that Jesus would have been brought up with included:

■ **Fasting:** abstaining from food to devote time to prayer. Fasting was common in Judaism, as we see in the Old Testament, and Jesus himself fasted (Matthew 4:2). While his presence was a reason more for feasting than fasting, he foresaw a day coming when his followers would fast once again (Mark 2:18–20).

■ **Tithing:** giving one-tenth of your income to God (Leviticus 27:30–32; Numbers 18:21–32) as an expression of gratitude and dependence. While a requirement of the Law, both Abraham and Isaac tithed long before the Law was given, simply as a spontaneous expression of their hearts. Jesus never criticized tithing, only people's wrong attitudes in doing it (Matthew 23:23).

■ **Sabbath:** the weekly rest day, marked by stopping all routine work to be refreshed and remember God's rest after creation (Exodus 20:8). Jesus would criticize the legalistic way this was implemented.

Jesus often challenged contemporary interpretations of these practices because they had become buried under man-made traditions which had become more important than the underlying principle itself.

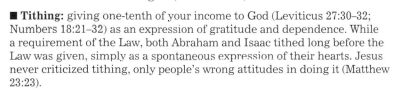

KEY SAYING

"'Love the Lord your God with all your heart and with all your soul and with all your mind." This is the first and greatest commandment. And the second is like it: "Love your neighbour as yourself."'

MATTHEW 22:37–39

His Preparation
THE STAGE IS SET

Before any royal visit, a messenger would be sent ahead, calling everyone to prepare for the king's coming. Over 700 years earlier, Isaiah had prophesied that the Messiah would send such a messenger ahead of him, also calling people to get ready. That messenger was John the Baptist, whose ministry signalled that Jesus' final steps of preparation were here: his work was almost ready to begin.

John the Baptist

John's parents had been childless; but an angel told Zechariah, a Temple priest, that Elizabeth would bear not just a child but Messiah's forerunner (Luke 1:5–25). When Mary, Jesus' mother, visited her relative Elizabeth, John leapt in her womb, prophetically anticipating his work of pointing to Jesus, who even then was in Mary's womb. Since John's parents were elderly, they may have died while he was young, leaving him to be adopted by the Qumran community, which had priestly connections and often adopted. If so, it explains similarities in their messages.

John's ministry centred on 'a baptism of repentance for the forgiveness of sins' (Mark 1:4). His call to a repentance matched by lifestyle (Luke 3:7–18) wasn't, in itself, unusual; many Old Testament prophets had done the same. What was shocking was John's insistence on marking this by baptism, something Jews demanded only of Gentile converts. So John was in effect saying that Jews too were outsiders! It was this practice that earned him the name 'the Baptizer' or 'the Baptist'. Hundreds of ordinary people responded to his message, but the religious leaders were offended by it (Matthew 3:7–10; Luke 3:7–9).

John was finally imprisoned in the Machaerus fortress for criticizing Herod Antipas's incestuous marriage to Herodias, his brother's wife, where he was beheaded as a birthday gift to Salome (Matthew 14:1–12).

How Old Was Jesus?

Two pieces of evidence help us establish Jesus' age when he began his ministry:

■ Early in his ministry, Jewish leaders reminded him that the Temple had taken forty-six years to build (John 2:20). Since its construction began in 19 BC, that gives a date of around AD 27 for the start of Jesus' ministry.

■ Luke dates the beginning of John's ministry as the fifteenth year of Tiberius, which gives a date of AD 29.

Since Jesus was born in 5 BC, that means he was around thirty-two to thirty-four years old when he began his ministry, which fits well, in that culture of those times, with Luke's statement that Jesus was 'about thirty years old when he began his ministry' (Luke 3:23).

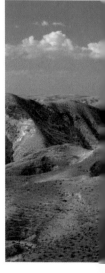

JESUS' BAPTISM

Jesus' first step of preparation was to go to the Jordan to be baptized by John (Matthew 3:13–17; Mark 1:9–11; Luke 3:21–22; John 1:29–34). Despite John's reluctance, Jesus humbly identified with God's people, modelling the need to turn to God afresh as John was calling for, even though he himself was God's Son. As he was baptized, God confirmed his calling in a special way: the Holy Spirit came on him and a voice declared he was indeed God's Son.

While early icons portray Jesus standing waist-deep in the river with John pouring water over him, his baptism was almost certainly by immersion. The very word 'baptize' means 'immerse', and only this kind of baptism makes sense of Paul's description of it as a burial of one's old life (Romans 6:3–7).

... a voice of one calling in the desert, 'Prepare the way of the LORD, make straight paths for him.'

MARK 1:3

● SEE ALSO
FASTING PP. 29, 74
QUMRAN P. 18
RIVER JORDAN P. 15

Wilderness Temptations

After his baptism Jesus was led by God's Spirit into the wilderness where he spent forty days praying, fasting and being tempted by the devil. Centuries earlier, Israel had been led by God through the Sinai wilderness on their way from Egypt to the Promised Land and had faced many tests and trials, but had failed them all; here now was the man representing the new Israel who would also face tests, but triumph.

In facing these temptations, Jesus resolved some issues at the outset of his ministry:

■ He would not resort to 'quick fixes' but would do things God's way, depending solely on him and his word. His quoting Scripture (all from Deuteronomy, the book of Israel's wilderness years) shows his high view of its authority and power.

■ He would remain obedient to God, unlike Adam, who had failed the test of obedience.

■ He would not pursue a worldly form of messiahship, gathering followers by signs and establishing God's kingdom by force, but would walk the path of humility.

■ He would overcome the devil, exposing his claims to rule this earth for the empty lies that they were.

The Desert Fathers

The attraction of the wilderness as a place of retreat from the world appealed to a group in the early church known as the Desert Fathers. The movement began in Egypt when St Anthony went to live alone in the desert around AD 280. The movement soon spread to Palestine, with its obvious attraction as the place where Jesus too spent time in the desert. Two different patterns of monastic life developed: some monks lived alone in caves while others lived communally; but both followed a pattern of prayer, reading Scripture and manual work. The movement ended in AD 614 when Persia invaded Palestine. Some monasteries sprang up again later.

An aerial view of the monastery of Qarantal in the Judean Desert, located 6.8 miles (11 km) east of Jericho.

JUDEAN DESERT

Pictured is the Judean desert where John preached. Deserts had played a key role in Israel's history, and the prophets said Messiah would come from here (e.g. Isaiah 40:3–5), so it was little wonder huge crowds gathered when John started preaching there (Matthew 3:5). John lived an ascetic lifestyle, wearing rough clothes and eating locusts and wild honey (Mark 1:6), all deliberately prophetic, for Elijah had lived a similar lifestyle and his reappearance was expected before Messiah came (Malachi 4:5–6).

KEY SAYING

'We must do all that God wants us to do.'

MATTHEW 3:15

His Launch
RECEPTION AND REJECTION

The preparation over, it was time to begin. Jesus returned to Galilee and started his ministry, though with mixed results. While some received his message gladly, others weren't so happy; and in Nazareth, his home town, he was rejected as a young upstart. These mixed reactions would be prophetic of what the next three years would hold for him.

JESUS' FIRST MIRACLE

Jesus' first miracle occurred in a surprising setting: a wedding (John 2:1–11), underlining his concern not just for the 'religious' bits of life, but for every aspect. It happened in the obscure village of Cana near Nazareth. Weddings lasted a week and the whole village was invited, so it's not surprising they ran out of wine. Jesus, one of the guests, came to the rescue by miraculously transforming water into wine; and not just any wine, but the best they had ever tasted.

But this miracle was about far more than rescuing the host from embarrassment; the six large stone water jars were used for ceremonial washing and now, by turning their water into wine, Jesus had made them 'unclean' and useless. John describes this miracle as a 'sign': a pointer to a deeper truth. Like the water jars, Judaism itself had become useless and needed replacing; and the man with the 'new wine' of God's kingdom was right there with them, demonstrating God's abundant generosity and transforming power.

JESUS BEGINS HIS MINISTRY

While it is impossible to be absolutely certain about the chronology of Jesus' ministry, the early months probably looked something like this:

1. Left his childhood home.

2. Baptized by John.

3. Tempted by the devil.

4. First miracle performed at a wedding.

5. Temple visited and cleansed.

6. Encountered a Samaritan woman.

7. Rejected in Nazareth.

8. Moved to new base in Capernaum.

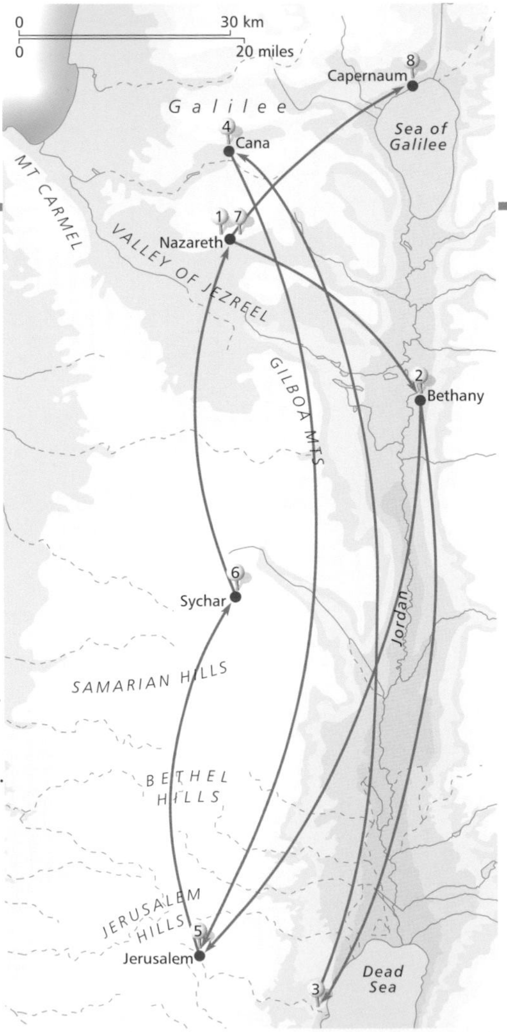

A Samaritan Woman

Jesus decided to take the direct route back to Galilee, through Samaria, rather than the longer route east of the Jordan preferred by devout Jews who felt that passing through Samaria defiled them. His lengthy conversation with a Samaritan woman, which broke social taboos, shocked his followers when they returned; but they would find many more taboos broken in the coming months. The encounter changed her life and led to many Samaritans believing in Jesus (John 4:1–41). Here was an early indication that his message wasn't just for Jews, but for all who opened their hearts to him.

Map labels: 0 — 30 km / 0 — 20 miles; Capernaum 8; Galilee; Cana 4; Sea of Galilee; MT CARMEL; VALLEY OF JEZREEL; Nazareth 1 7; Bethany 2; GILBOA MTS; Sychar 6; Jordan; SAMARIAN HILLS; BETHEL HILLS; JERUSALEM HILLS; Jerusalem 5; Dead Sea 3

Jesus returned to Galilee in the power of the Spirit.
LUKE 4:14

● SEE ALSO
LAKE GALILEE P. 15
NAZARETH P. 27
TEMPLE P. 17

CLEANSING THE TEMPLE

When Jesus visited the Jerusalem Temple at Passover, he was shocked by what he found: merchants and money-changers had turned the Courtyard of the Gentiles into a marketplace. While animals needed to be sold for sacrifices and currency needed to be exchanged (for only Temple currency, without images, could be used there), commercial activities were so dominating this outer courtyard that it was impossible for Gentiles to pray. Jesus was angry, saying, 'How dare you turn my Father's house into a market!' (John 2:16). Making a whip from cords, he drove out the animals and upturned the money-changers' tables.

John places this story after the wedding at Cana to underline that Jesus had come to transform Judaism, and not even its most sacred spot, the Temple, was exempt. Matthew, Mark and Luke, however, place the Temple cleansing at the end of Jesus' ministry. So either John moved the story to highlight what Jesus' ministry was all about, or there were two Temple cleansings. After all, vested interests are hard to break, especially where money is concerned; so it isn't hard to imagine these practices creeping back over three years.

Rejection in Nazareth

While Jesus met with initial popularity (Luke 4:15), his message soon alienated as many as it attracted. This was certainly true in his home town of Nazareth, where he was invited to read the Scriptures and preach in the synagogue one Sabbath (Luke 4:16–30). He read from Isaiah's prophecy of Messiah bringing God's new age of freedom (Isaiah 61:1–2). So far, so good; everybody believed that. But when he then claimed, 'Today this scripture is fulfilled in your hearing' (Luke 4:21) – that is, that God's new age of freedom had begun through him – the atmosphere started to change. When he then gave hope to Gentiles through the Old Testament stories he quoted, it was the final straw: they drove him out of town and tried to throw him off a cliff. But he miraculously escaped and left Nazareth, never to return.

Perhaps surprisingly in the light of the town's response, Jesus was often known as 'Jesus of Nazareth' (e.g. Matthew 21:11; Mark 1:24; Luke 18:37; John 18:5; 19:19).

Capernaum

Rejected in Nazareth, Jesus moved to Capernaum (Kephar Nahum, 'the village of Nahum'), a town of probably fewer than 1,500 inhabitants alongside the Sea of Galilee. Several towns, some of them quite large, had sprung up around this freshwater lake because of the fishing industry it supported, and it was here that Jesus based his work for the next three years.

His relocation to Capernaum was quite strategic. The main north–south highway skirted the town, which lay close to the border with Gaulanitis, creating a fair amount of commercial activity. So while Capernaum was probably relatively quiet in parts, it was also relatively influential, an ideal base for Jesus' ministry, therefore, and a place to which he often returned after ministry elsewhere. He saw it, and especially Peter's house, as 'home', something anyone who travels a lot will know the importance of.

Ruins of the synagogue at Capernaum dating from the fourth century, though excavations show it stands on the site of the synagogue from Jesus' time.

KEY SAYING

'No prophet is accepted in his hometown.'

LUKE 4:24

His Disciples
CALLED TO FOLLOW

Jesus had already been teaching and healing for some time before he called his disciples, which may explain their prompt abandonment of everything to follow him: they had probably already seen him in action, or at least heard of him. But now, in choosing twelve, Jesus was doing more than calling disciples; he was establishing a new people of God. And these ragamuffin characters he called were the ones through whom he would do it.

Tabgha, the traditional location of Jesus' calling of Simon Peter and Andrew. As he walked further along the beach, he saw two other brothers, James and John, preparing their nets and called them too. He promised they would all be catching people from now on.

The Twelve

From among his many followers, Jesus chose just twelve to be his disciples (or 'apprentices'). He called them 'apostles' (Mark 3:14), meaning 'representatives' or 'messengers', and appointed them 'that they might be with him and that he might send them out to preach and to have authority to drive out demons' (Mark 3:14–15). The twelve would certainly have failed most job interviews today, being men of little education, few prospects and, in some cases, dubious character and background. These twelve were:

- **Simon Peter:** hot-headed fisherman from Capernaum
- **James:** fisherman from Capernaum
- **John:** fisherman and James's brother
- **Andrew:** fisherman and Peter's brother
- **Philip:** from Bethsaida, perhaps of Greek background
- **Bartholomew:** also called Nathaniel, a straightforward man
- **Matthew:** tax collector
- **Thomas:** famous for doubting the resurrection
- **James:** son of Alphaeus, about whom little is known
- **Thaddaeus:** also called Judas
- **Simon the Zealot:** former nationalist freedom-fighter
- **Judas Iscariot:** group treasurer who would betray Jesus

Besides this inner core, Jesus had a wider group of followers (Luke 10:1), including women (highly unusual, if not scandalous, in those days), some of whom supported him financially (Luke 8:2–3). This cross-section of society was prophetic of God's new people that Jesus had come to establish.

Why Twelve?

The Gospels show that Jesus had far more than twelve followers and that this wider group included both men and women. So why choose this inner group of twelve, and why only men? It was Jesus' way of making a deliberately prophetic statement. When Israel was founded, it had been built around the twelve sons of Jacob (also called Israel), who were 'patriarchs' – father-rulers who led their families and clans. From these would develop the twelve tribes that made up Israel, the people of God. In choosing twelve men as his apostles, therefore, Jesus was saying he was founding a new Israel, a new people of God, built around him, and in whom the promises of the Old Testament would now be fulfilled.

They pulled their boats up on shore, left everything and followed him.
LUKE 5:11

Peter's Call

Simon Peter had first encountered Jesus when he healed his mother-in-law (Luke 4:38–39). This must have made a big impact on him, though it didn't lead to him immediately following Jesus. That happened some time later. Peter and his workmates were washing their nets after a night's fruitless fishing when Jesus asked to use one of their boats as a floating pulpit (Luke 5:1–5). The sermon over, he paid for its hire with a miracle. He told them to re-cast their nets, even though these experienced fishermen had caught nothing all night, and daytime (when fish could see the nets) certainly wasn't the time to start again. Nevertheless, perhaps encouraged by the healing of his mother-in-law, Peter did what Jesus said. Suddenly, the nets were full to breaking, and they needed the others to come and help. This transformation of Peter's world made him suddenly aware of his sinfulness; but Jesus responded with encouragement, not judgment. 'Don't be afraid; from now on you will catch men' (Luke 5:10).

Peter would become a key leader in the group and one of Jesus' closest friends. His hot-headedness wouldn't disappear overnight (John 18:10), and his fear of people would be a constant weakness (Luke 22:54–61; Galatians 2:11–13); yet this was the man to whom Jesus said, 'You are Peter, and on this rock I will build my church' (Matthew 16:18). While the Bible is silent about his later life, church tradition says he ended up in Rome where he was executed for his Christian faith.

PETER'S HOUSE

The likely ruins of Peter's house in Capernaum. Graffiti shows Christian association with this house from the second century, and in the fifth century a large Byzantine church was built over it.

The hull of a boat recovered from the mud of the north-western shore of Lake Galilee. Dating from the first century AD, it is 25.5 feet (8 m) long and 7.5 feet (2.3 m) wide and is typical of the boats used in Jesus' day. It would have had a crew of around four to five.

Tax Collectors

Matthew belonged to one of the most hated sectors of society: tax collectors. While never loved in any society, in Palestine they were particularly hated, being seen as both corrupt and collaborators. By paying money in advance to the Roman occupiers, they purchased the right to collect taxes for a particular district, but then made massive profits through hugely inflated assessments of taxable items, with Roman soldiers enforcing their demands. Matthew would have been quite wealthy since Capernaum was a key trading place and border post. He would also have been fluent in Greek as a tax officer, something that would be very useful for writing his Gospel later.

Jesus' invitation to Matthew to become a disciple was just one example of how he would reach out to despised, outcast or hated groups in society.

KEY SAYING

'Come, follow me… and I will make you fishers of men.'
MARK 1:17

His Teaching: God
THE GRACIOUS FATHER

If there was one thing that marked out Jesus more than anything else, it was his view of God. While at one level it was completely orthodox, at another it was utterly radical, transforming the scribes' and Pharisees' vision of a demanding God into one of him as a gracious and forgiving Father whose love reached everyone. The surprising thing was, this vision wasn't new; it was all in the Old Testament, if only his opponents had opened their eyes to see.

The Father

Jesus' favourite term of address for God was 'Father', used 168 times. For his opponents this was blasphemous, because while Israel and its kings were described as God's 'son' in the Old Testament, no individual would ever dare call God 'Father' like Jesus did. It so outraged his critics that they 'tried all the harder to kill him... he was even calling God his own Father, making himself equal with God' (John 5:18). This intimacy was pushed even further when Jesus called God *Abba*, the Aramaic for 'daddy' (Mark 14:36), almost certainly a unique form of address to God in those days. Jesus encouraged his followers to see God as their heavenly Father too (e.g. Matthew 6:9), and they would retain the word '*Abba*' even when Christianity moved from Aramaic-speaking Palestine into the Greek-speaking world (Romans 8:15; Galatians 4:6), showing how deeply loved this title had become.

Detail from a ceiling painting depicting *The Fall of the Rebel Angels*, by Giacinto Brandi, 1677–79.

The God of Jesus

People sometimes try to drive a wedge between Jesus' view of God and that of the Old Testament; but this simply can't be done. The God that Jesus believed in *was* the God of the Old Testament: creative, majestic, awesome, holy, righteous. Yet the same Old Testament also taught he was 'the LORD, the LORD, the compassionate and gracious God, slow to anger, abounding in love and faithfulness, maintaining love to thousands, and forgiving wickedness, rebellion and sin' (Exodus 34:6–7). Religious leaders of Jesus' day also believed this, but only for them and their kind: those who fulfilled the Jewish Law and so deserved it. But Jesus taught that God's love went much further, reaching out to those who *didn't* deserve it, drawing them in to himself and the new people of God he was forming. And he demonstrated this, not just through teaching, but through healing the sick, forgiving sinners, welcoming everyone and sharing meals with whoever would invite him.

The Prodigal Son

One of Jesus' best-known parables is the prodigal son (Luke 15:11–32), though it might be better called 'the parable of the forgiving father' since this is its key idea. A son who demands, then wastes, his family inheritance is reduced to herding pigs (for Jews, unclean animals). Coming to his senses, he returns to his father, seeking his forgiveness. Rather than receiving the scolding he expected, he finds the father welcomes him with open arms and throws a party. Everyone is happy – except his older brother (representing the scribes and Pharisees) who had stayed home, working hard and being a good boy. He feels his brother has been treated better than he deserves – and that is exactly Jesus' point of course; because that is what God is like.

We have seen his glory, the glory of the One and Only, who came from the Father, full of grace and truth.

JOHN 1:14

VINEYARD WORKERS

Jesus' view of God as kind, merciful and gracious comes out in the parable of the workers in the vineyard (Matthew 20:1–16). It's harvest time, and the vineyard owner goes out early in the morning to hire day-labourers, agreeing to pay them the usual day's wage of a denarius. But all through the day – at 9 a.m., noon and 3 p.m. – he keeps returning to the marketplace and, finding men hanging around doing nothing, sends them to join the others, promising them a fair reward. Even at 5 p.m., he's still inviting men to come and work. At the end of the day, it's pay time. Starting with those hired last, he gives them a denarius – a full day's wage for only an hour's work! No doubt the others are thinking that they will get even more; but to their huge disappointment, they're given exactly the same and start to grumble. The master reminds them he isn't being unfair to them (after all, he gave them what he promised); he's simply being more than fair to the others.

In this parable Jesus revealed God's amazing grace, as abundant to those who come last as to those who come first. The only people who didn't like such teaching were the religious leaders, who felt they had been 'working hard all day' by their strict observance of the Law and therefore deserved far more than others. But Jesus turned their vision of God on its head.

FATHER KNOWS

'Are not two sparrows sold for a penny? Yet not one of them will fall to the ground apart from the will of your Father. And even the very hairs of your head are all numbered. So don't be afraid; you are worth more than many sparrows' (Matthew 10:29–31).

Knowing God as Father was not, for Jesus, an academic matter; it was meant to bring people a sense of security in God's protection and confidence in his provision (Matthew 6:7–8, 25–34). The solution to every situation was: don't panic; Father knows. Jesus himself would live in this confidence throughout his life, even when soldiers finally came to arrest him (Matthew 26:53–54).

KEY SAYING

'If you, then, though you are evil, know how to give good gifts to your children, how much more will your Father in heaven give good gifts to those who ask him!'

MATTHEW 7:11

His Teaching: God's Kingdom
THE FUTURE STARTS NOW

Contrary to popular thinking, Jesus' teaching wasn't primarily about God's love, but about God's kingdom. His fellow-Jews believed in that kingdom; but for them, it was something wholly in the future. Jesus put a shocking spin on things, however, saying that it was already here. The future was starting right now. 'The time has come... The kingdom of God is near. Repent and believe the good news!' (Mark 1:15). This good news wasn't that people were sinners (hardly good news!); it was that God's kingdom was here and that it was for them.

What is God's Kingdom?

We think of a kingdom as a place; but that's not what Jesus meant. The Greek word for kingdom means 'rule' rather than 'realm', the activity of ruling rather than the place ruled. God's kingdom is therefore God's rule, and Jesus came to show what living under that rule looked like. While Jews felt this kingdom was something for the future, Jesus said it had pushed dynamically into the present age right now, like a volcanic eruption that would completely change the landscape.

Matthew calls it 'the kingdom of heaven' rather than 'the kingdom of God' because he was writing for people from a Jewish background who avoided using God's name, feeling it was too holy. So he used the common periphrasis 'heaven' instead.

SEEKING THE KINGDOM

'The kingdom of heaven is like treasure hidden in a field. When a man found it, he hid it again, and then in his joy went and sold all he had and bought that field' (Matthew 13:44).

The thing about hidden treasure is that it is as near to the person who found it as the person who missed it. No doubt the farmer had ploughed that field many times, children had played in it often, travellers had crossed it many times, yet they had all missed the treasure. That's what God's kingdom is like, Jesus said: so near and yet, without 'finding' it, so far. It's hidden, but God wants us to find it. To find it, however, we really need to look.

Demonstrating the Kingdom

Jesus didn't simply describe the kingdom, he demonstrated it. That's why Mark opens his Gospel with a string of stories showing the extent of Jesus' kingly rule. He demonstrates his authority over:

- Demons (1:21–28)
- Disease (1:29–34)
- Uncleanness (1:40–45)
- Paralysis and sin (2:1–12)
- Social exclusion (2:13–17)
- Religious tradition and rules (2:18 – 3:5)

Eternal Life

In John's Gospel God's kingdom is mentioned just three times (John 3:3, 5; 18:36); but the concept is there much more, for Jesus speaks about 'eternal life', meaning far more than 'life that lasts forever'. It literally means 'life of the eternal age', the life of God's age-to-come which can start to be experienced right now. It was this sort of life that Jesus challenged Nicodemus, a leading religious figure, to discover for himself (John 3:1–21).

Jesus went throughout Galilee, teaching in their synagogues, preaching the good news of the kingdom, and healing every disease and sickness among the people.

MATTHEW 4:23

● SEE ALSO
HIS AUTHORITY PP. 66–67
PARABLES P. 64
JESUS' RETURN P. 120

The Kingdom's Challenge

The kingdom is worth everything, Jesus said, but it also demands everything. That's why he called his disciples to leave everything and follow him (Mark 1:17) and why others would meet similar challenges from him (Luke 18:18–30).

God's kingdom isn't something we're born into, no matter what spiritual pedigree we might claim (John 8:39); it's something we must choose to enter, paying whatever it costs (Matthew 16:24–25), entering by the narrow door which is too small for all life's clutter (Matthew 7:13–14). And once we've entered, we have to trust God like little children trust their parents (Matthew 18:3).

A CLASH OF TWO KINGDOMS

From the outset it was clear that Jesus would encounter conflict, both with human kingdoms (reflected in Herod's attempt to kill him, Matthew 2:1–18) and spiritual ones (reflected in the devil's tempting him, Matthew 4:1–11). Jesus was deeply aware of this clash of two kingdoms and trained his disciples to overcome it (Luke 10:17–20). The conflict would climax at the cross, when human and spiritual powers came together to destroy him. But God's kingdom would prove more powerful, as the resurrection would show.

While the struggle would continue (Matthew 24:1–35), God's kingdom would ultimately prevail at the return of Jesus (Matthew 24:36 – 25:46).

This picture of *The Temptation of Christ on the Mountain* by Duccio di Buoninsegna depicts the clash of the kingdoms.

A Kingdom for All

The Old Testament often expressed the future triumph of God's kingdom as a victory banquet for his people (e.g. Isaiah 25:6–9). Invited by a leading Pharisee to a meal, Jesus took the opportunity to teach about this 'messianic banquet', but with an unexpected twist (Luke 14:1–24). While Isaiah had prophesied that 'all nations' would be present at it, by Jesus' time Jews no longer believed this; but Jesus said that there would be lots of surprises at the End. When the host in Jesus' parable found his invited guests wouldn't come, he turned their insult into an opportunity for grace, inviting outcasts to come instead and leaving the original invitees outside – a real shock to his Pharisee audience.

THE KINGDOM'S TRIUMPH

'What shall I compare the kingdom of God to? It is like yeast that a woman took and mixed into a large amount of flour until it worked all through the dough' (Luke 13:20–21).

Just as yeast has effects disproportionate to its size, so does God's kingdom. From insignificant beginnings it will one day permeate everything. Other images used to describe this triumphant kingdom include (from Matthew 13):

■ Seed that grows despite all hindrances

■ A tiny mustard seed that becomes the biggest plant

■ Treasure worth selling everything for

■ A net catching all kinds of fish

■ Treasure brought from a storeroom

KEY SAYING

'Seek first his kingdom and his righteousness, and all these things will be given to you as well.'

MATTHEW 6:33

His Teaching: Discipleship
LEARNING FOR LIFE

Jesus wasn't interested in people becoming 'Christians'; he wanted them to be 'disciples'. Simply being a Christian – believing certain things about him – wasn't enough. He was looking for a dynamic change of heart, attitude and vision in people that would draw them into his mission of forming the new people of God. Discipleship was his chosen tool for bringing about this transformation.

What is Discipleship?

Discipleship (apprenticeship or mentoring) was very common in Jesus' time. Someone wanting to learn the skills of another (whether craftsman, rabbi or philosopher) would become his disciple, at first listening, watching and learning, but then gradually doing it themselves until the skills or knowledge were fully transferred. So in many ways, Jesus wasn't doing anything radical by having disciples. But whereas normally apprentices sought out a teacher, Jesus turned the process on its head: he, the teacher, went and found the apprentices he wanted.

The disciples' first priority was spending time with him, getting to know him and understanding his heart, and then out of that, joining his mission (Mark 3:14). Jesus' discipleship wasn't just about teaching, but involving them in his work, encouraging them when they got things right (Matthew 16:13–20), correcting them (Matthew 16:21–28) or helping them when they got things wrong (Matthew 17:14–21), and ultimately sending them out to 'have a go' themselves (Luke 9:1–6, 10).

'Come to me, all you who are weary and burdened, and I will give you rest. Take my yoke upon you and learn from me, for I am gentle and humble in heart, and you will find rest for your souls. For my yoke is easy and my burden is light' (Matthew 11:28–30).

Paradoxically, Jesus promised people rest by telling them to pick up a burden. But it was not the burden of obedience to the many rules of the Pharisees, which he went on to challenge (Matthew 12:1–13), but rather the yoke of obedience to him, which was liberating. Just as younger oxen would be paired in a yoke with older oxen to train them, so Jesus calls his followers to team up with him and learn about life.

> 'Disciple' is the normal word in the New Testament for a follower of Jesus, used 282 times. By contrast, the word 'believer' is used just twenty-six times and 'Christian' just three times.

Accountability

While few of us love accountability, Jesus wrote it into his discipleship programme, teaching it as a principle, like in the parable of the talents (Matthew 25:14–30), and following it as a practice, like when he sent his disciples out on mission (Luke 9:1–2, 10; 10:1–4, 17). Jesus commended the Roman centurion for his understanding of authority and accountability, saying he showed remarkable faith (Matthew 8:5–10).

The Sphere of Discipleship

Jesus was not content with mentoring his disciples in just spiritual matters; the whole of life came into it, including:

- Character (Matthew 5:1–12)
- Attitudes (Mark 10:35–45)
- Fears (Matthew 6:25–34)
- Behaviour (Matthew 6:1–4)
- Money (Luke 16:10–12)
- Relationships (Matthew 18:15–35)
- Prayer (Luke 11:1–4)
- Fruitfulness (John 15:1–16)

In ministry he frequently pushed the disciples onto the edge of their faith, like when he told *them* to distribute five loaves and two fish to a crowd of thousands (Matthew 14:19).

The disciples went and did as Jesus had instructed them.
MATTHEW 21:6

● SEE ALSO
DISCIPLES P. 34
HIS TEACHING PP. 36–59
THE DESERT FATHERS P. 31

The Monastic Movement

Monasteries are one particular expression of Christian discipleship. Originating in remote parts of Syria and Egypt in the third century, they were attempts to get away from the busyness and corruption of a sinful world in order to devote oneself to a life of discipline and prayer. Members submitted themselves to their 'Monastic Rule' (rules governing their way of life) and lived in community, sharing whatever worldly goods they had. The model caught on in the Western church, spreading rapidly in the fifth and sixth centuries. One of the best-known monastic founders was Augustine of Hippo, who established the Augustinians. Although by the time of the Reformation some monasteries and nunneries had become very lax, if not downright sinful, they were originally great centres of mission, study and prayer, as many continue to be today. This picture shows the Agias Triados Monastery in Greece.

MATURITY AND FRUITFULNESS

The goal of Jesus' discipleship was to bring his disciples into maturity and fruitfulness. He wanted every disciple to be 'like his master' (Matthew 10:25), fruitful (John 15:16) and doing the works he did and even greater works (John 14:11–12). The apostle Paul too saw church leaders' primary role as being 'to prepare God's people for works of service, so that the body of Christ may be built up until we all reach unity in the faith and in the knowledge of the Son of God and become mature, attaining to the whole measure of the fullness of Christ' (Ephesians 4:12–13).

'The harvest is plentiful, but the workers are few. Ask the Lord of the harvest, therefore, to send out workers into his harvest field' (Luke 10:2).

For Jesus the goal of discipleship was sending workers into the harvest field of people which he saw as ripe for harvesting.

Discipleship: The Final Word

Matthew's Gospel ends with Jesus telling his followers: 'Go and make disciples of all nations' (Matthew 28:19). Luke's second volume, the book of Acts, begins with similar words: 'You will… be my witnesses in Jerusalem, and in all Judea and Samaria, and to the ends of the earth' (Acts 1:8). In both accounts the final burden of Jesus before returning to heaven was for his disciples to go and make other disciples.

KEY SAYING

'If anyone would come after me, he must deny himself and take up his cross and follow me.'

MARK 8:34

His Teaching: Repentance
THE CHALLENGE TO CHANGE

Jesus came preaching good news, not bad news: the good news that God's kingdom was here. But his good news wasn't some woolly message that God loved us and therefore everything would somehow be okay. The good news needed responding to; it demanded change, the most profound change of a person's life: repentance – nothing less than a deep-seated reorientation of the whole of life that opened the door to God's kingdom.

What is Repentance?

The Greek word used in the Gospels for 'repentance' is *metanoia*, meaning 'turning' – a change of heart and mind that produces a *turning from* our sinful ways, and a *turning to* God in love and obedience. Unlike the religious leaders, however, Jesus didn't teach the need for Temple sacrifice as an essential aspect of this repentance, because he understood his own sacrifice would become the basis of it. This apparently casual attitude towards the traditional means of repentance earned him the dismissive title 'friend of sinners' (Luke 7:34).

Case Study 1: Zacchaeus (Luke 19)

When Zacchaeus, the regional tax collector, heard Jesus was passing through Jericho, he wanted to see him. After all, this was the biggest thing to hit town since Cleopatra had visited seventy years earlier. His small height and an unco-operative crowd meant he couldn't get a decent view, however, so he climbed into a sycamore-fig tree. Jesus spotted him and invited himself home for dinner. Zacchaeus was delighted (verse 6) since, as a tax collector, he probably had few friends; but the crowds were disgusted with what Jesus did (verse 7).

We aren't told what they discussed; but by the end a profound change had happened in Zacchaeus, and he was offering half his possessions to the poor and a fourfold repayment on overcharging (news of which probably spread like wildfire). While there had been no 'prayer of repentance' as such, Jesus believed it had happened, saying, 'Today salvation has come to this house' (verse 9). Zacchaeus had come to repentance, not through judgmental words, but through kindness and acceptance.

A sycamore-fig tree whose low branches would have made it easy for a short man like Zacchaeus to climb.

JERICHO

Jericho lay some 850 feet (260 m) below sea level, which is why Herod the Great built a winter palace there since its climate was more pleasant than Jerusalem's, which was almost 2,500 feet (750 m) above sea level. Jericho was strategically located on the east–west road cutting through the northern and southern Judean hills, which meant much trade passed through – good news if you were a tax collector.

Jesus went into Galilee, proclaiming the good news of God. 'The time has come,' he said. 'The kingdom of God is near. Repent and believe the good news!'

MARK 1:14–15

Case Study 2: Nicodemus (John 3)

Nicodemus was a very senior religious figure. Coming to Jesus at night, perhaps wanting to get him alone or maybe because he was too embarrassed to come by day, he acknowledged him as a rabbi and miracle-worker (verse 2). But Jesus told him this wasn't enough to bring him into God's kingdom; he needed to be 'born again' or 'born from above' (verse 3). He explained to a perplexed Nicodemus, 'No-one can enter the kingdom of God unless he is born of water and the Spirit' (verse 5). In other words, being a good Jew (which is what Nicodemus's first, natural birth gave him) wasn't enough; he needed a second, spiritual birth through God's Spirit. Through this powerful image, Jesus showed the radical nature of the change needed to find a place in God's kingdom.

While the story doesn't tell us the outcome, it seems Nicodemus made that radical change and became a follower of Jesus. John tells us (19:38–42) that it was he, together with Joseph of Arimathea, who courageously buried Jesus and provided the 75 pounds (34 kg) of spices for anointing the body – a hugely costly gift.

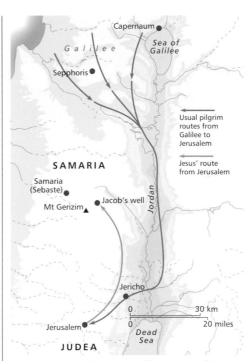

Case Study 3: A Samaritan Woman (John 4)

Most Jewish travellers avoided Samaria, even though it shortened the journey from Jerusalem to Galilee considerably, due to differences that went back five centuries but were still deeply felt. However, on one occasion Jesus deliberately chose to return that way (verse 4). Resting at Jacob's well while his followers went to buy food, he initiated a conversation with a Samaritan woman who had come for water, breaking the rules of Jewish piety and social custom. Jesus didn't preach at her but steadily drew her out, tantalizingly offering her 'living water' (verse 10). He then gently exposed her loose moral lifestyle, which God had revealed to him (verses 16–18). Her attempts to deflect him through theological debate (verses 19–20) were gently pushed aside until she finally realized she had probably found the Messiah (verse 29). We're not specifically told that she repented, but it seems quite likely since many Samaritans certainly did so because of her testimony (verses 39–40).

Making It Easy

The scribes and Pharisees made repentance hard, especially for non-religious people; but these were the very people Jesus went to – 'sinners', tax collectors, prostitutes, even Gentiles. He wanted them to know that they could come to God just as they were, without jumping through religious hoops first. When the Pharisees sneered at Jesus for this he said, 'It is not the healthy who need a doctor, but the sick. I have not come to call the righteous, but sinners' (Mark 2:17).

'I tell you that in the same way there will be more rejoicing in heaven over one sinner who repents than over ninety-nine righteous persons who do not need to repent' (Luke 15:7) – the conclusion to Jesus' parable about a shepherd's joy in finding a lost sheep, reflecting God's joy over people who change.

KEY SAYING

'I tell you the truth, unless you change and become like little children, you will never enter the kingdom of heaven.'

MATTHEW 18:3

His Teaching: Love and Forgiveness
THE FORGIVEN FORGIVE

For Jesus, knowing and sharing God's love and forgiveness were life's greatest priorities. Of course, the religious leaders believed in God's love and forgiveness too; but only for them and their kind, not for 'sinners'. Yet these were the very people Jesus went to. Even on the cross, he was still forgiving: 'Father, forgive them, for they do not know what they are doing' (Luke 23:34). Here was a man who not only taught love and forgiveness, but practised it to the end.

The Greatest Commandment

A Pharisee once asked Jesus which was the greatest commandment (Mark 12:28–34). Jesus replied, like any good Jew would, 'The most important one is this: "Hear, O Israel, the Lord our God, the Lord is one. Love the Lord your God with all your heart and with all your soul and with all your mind and with all your strength"' (verses 29–30). But then he added, 'The second is this: "Love your neighbour as yourself." There is no commandment greater than these' (verse 31). Jesus was asked for the one greatest commandment, but his reply gave two, thereby inextricably linking love for God with love for one's neighbour, as underlined in the parable of the good Samaritan (Luke 10:25–37).

The Motivation of Love

Reading the Gospels, it's impossible to miss that Jesus' constant motivation was love for people, especially those nobody else loved; those who couldn't keep the religious rules, who'd messed up their lives, who were outcasts, who'd fallen into sin. In fact, he preferred spending time with these rather than with religious leaders. Yet his love wasn't sentimental, allowing people to do what they wanted; it was so impacting that he could also challenge them to leave their life of sin.

Forgiven and Forgiving

Jesus said that the forgiven need also to be forgiving. Unforgiveness is more than ingratitude to God; it is a prison that locks us up, from which it is difficult to escape, as Jesus taught in the parable of the unforgiving servant (Matthew 18:21–35). Forgiving others therefore takes priority even over going to worship (Matthew 5:23–26).

The Golden Rule

Not doing to others what you wouldn't want them to do to you is a 'golden rule' in many societies. A contemporary of Jesus, Rabbi Hillel, put it like this: 'What is hateful to you, do not do to your fellow creature. That is the whole Law; all else is explanation.' But that was too 'safe' a philosophy for Jesus. For him, love was far more dynamic; so he taught: '*Do to others what you would have them do to you*' (Matthew 7:12).

Leprosy was common in Bible times, though it probably included skin conditions wider than modern leprosy, which is characterized by skin lesions, loss of feeling, muscle weakness and deformity.

Because it could be contagious, Jewish Law required lepers to keep in social isolation (Leviticus 13:45–46); but Jesus chose to spend time with them. Indeed many of his healings concerned lepers or others with bad skin diseases, perhaps because it was an expected sign of the Messianic Age, as Jesus reminded John the Baptist when he doubted (Matthew 11:2–6).

● SEE ALSO
HIS CRUCIFIXION P. 102
GOOD SAMARITAN P. 65
PRODIGAL SON P. 36

Authority to Forgive

A paralysed man was once brought by his friends to be healed by Jesus (Mark 2:1–12). They were so desperate that, finding the house packed, they climbed onto the flat mud roof, dug a hole through it and lowered him down. Jesus' first response wasn't to heal him, however, but to say, 'Son, your sins are forgiven' (verse 5). The scribes were outraged by this blasphemous claim, for only God could forgive sins (verses 6–7). But Jesus then gave them another problem, healing the man 'that you may know that the Son of man has authority on earth to forgive sins' (verse 10). Here was claim backed up by action.

LOVING ENEMIES

Jesus said we shouldn't just forgive our friends; after all, any fool can do that. True love reaches beyond our feelings to forgive even our enemies (Matthew 5:43–48; Luke 6:27–36).

In contrast to the Pharisees, who were afraid of contamination through eating with the 'wrong' sort of people, Jesus would eat with anyone. By engaging in such 'table fellowship' Jesus showed his acceptance of people just as they were, without requiring them to put things right with God *first*.

A Forgiven Woman

As in many countries still today, women got a rough deal in Jesus' day, which is perhaps why he showed particular concern for them. One example was when a woman mysteriously 'caught in the act of adultery' was brought to him for judgment (John 8:1–11), though he realized (since the man wasn't also brought) that it was him (Jesus) that was being set up as much as her. They reminded Jesus that the Law said she should be stoned (Leviticus 20:10); what did he say? If Jesus said, 'Stone her', where now was his love and forgiveness? If he forgave her, where was his respect for God's word? So he sat down and wrote in the dust – what he wrote, we aren't told. Perhaps he was simply doodling; perhaps he wrote 'Death', the penalty Moses prescribed (which would make sense of him then speaking of how it should be carried out). But then he said, 'If any one of you is without sin, let him be the first to throw a stone at her' (John 8:7), fulfilling the Law, yet making it impossible to be enacted. Her accusers gradually disappeared, their hostility now focused on Jesus. And then he told her to 'go and sin no more' – who knows, perhaps rubbing out the word in the dust as he did so.

KEY SAYING

'*A new command I give you: Love one another. As I have loved you, so you must love one another.*'

JOHN 13:34

His Teaching: Sermon on the Mount
KINGDOM LIFESTYLE

Possibly the best-known sermon in the world, the Sermon on the Mount is also the least understood. Often relegated at a popular level to 'nice thoughts, but impractical', or at a scholarly level to mere 'emergency regulations' from someone who thought 'the end' was close, Jesus' sermon is in fact for *all* his followers in *all* times: a blueprint for life in God's kingdom with its radical promises and demands.

The Beatitudes (Matthew 5:3–10)

Each Beatitude ('Blessing') begins with 'Blessed are...', or in today's language, 'Congratulations to...'. But each then seems far from being something to be congratulated for! Jesus was turning traditional values upside down; those who felt unblessed were about to experience God's blessing as his kingdom broke in – not through fighting God's enemies, as most Jews thought, but through humility and meekness.

Luke's version offers four blessings, counterbalanced by four woes.

Content

The Sermon on the Mount, as it was first called by Augustine (AD 354–430), a key church leader and theologian, is found in two different versions; a longer one (Matthew 5:1 – 7:29) and a shorter one (Luke 6:17–49). Some scholars think it was originally one sermon; others think it is a compilation, especially Matthew's version. However, both versions are almost identical in the order of their content, suggesting that one sermon originally lay behind it.

Matthew's version contains:

■ The Beatitudes (5:3–12)

■ A call to be salt and light (5:13–16)

■ Jesus' attitude to the Jewish Law (5:17–20)

■ Contrasts between the rabbis' teaching and his (5:21–48)

■ Teaching on giving, praying and fasting (6:1–18; 7:7–12)

■ Encouragements to put God first and trust him (6:19–34)

■ Ethical guidelines (7:1–6, 13–23)

■ The importance of acting upon Jesus' teaching (7:24–29)

The Mount of Beatitudes is the traditional location of the sermon. Visited by pilgrims since the fourth century, this site makes sense of Matthew's locating it 'on a mountainside' (Matthew 5:1) but Luke on a 'level place' (Luke 6:17); Luke's level place was a plateau on Matthew's hillside. The natural amphitheatre would have helped project Jesus' voice. The Franciscan Church of the Beatitudes was built on the site of fourth-century ruins with financial help from Mussolini. The chapel's octagonal shape represents the eight Beatitudes.

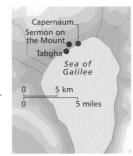

Location of the Sermon on the Mount, between Tabgha and Capernaum by the Sea of Galilee.

When he saw the crowds, he went up on a mountainside and sat down. His disciples came to him, and he began to teach them.

MATTHEW 5:1–2

● SEE ALSO
HIS ETHICS P. 68
KINGDOM OF GOD PP. 38–39
RABBI P. 74

A New Law?

The sermon is the first of five large blocks of teaching in Matthew (chapters 5–7, 10, 13, 18, 24–25), prompting some to think that Jesus saw his teaching as a 'new Law'; after all, it was delivered up a 'mountain' just like Moses' Law was (Exodus 19:3 – 20:21), and the five blocks of teaching perhaps reflect the five books of Moses (Genesis–Deuteronomy). However, while the sermon could be seen as a 'new Law', it's important to note that it comes in the context of 'good news' (Matthew 4:23). It is only as people respond to this, not by trying to keep laws, that they can embrace this radical lifestyle.

Who Was It For?

Because the sermon's demands are so exacting, people have interpreted it in various ways:

■ Nobel Peace Prize winner Albert Schweitzer thought it was so radical that Jesus could only have intended it as an 'interim ethic' for the short period that he thought Jesus envisaged between his death and the end of the age.

■ Catholic theologian Thomas Aquinas differentiated between its *commandments*, which all must keep to be saved, and its optional *counsels*, which were primarily for clergy rather than laity (though the sermon itself contains no such distinction).

■ Reformer Martin Luther's doctrine of 'the two realms', secular and spiritual, led him to believe that in the church, Christians must obey all the sermon's commands, but in society, natural law (common sense) must prevail – which comes dangerously close to allowing people to choose which parts of the sermon they want to obey!

However, the plain reading of the sermon is that Jesus saw this as the way of life for *all* his followers, in *every* area of life.

'You are the salt of the earth... you are the light of the world' (Matthew 5:13–14).

Jesus' followers are to make a difference, like salt that flavours and preserves, and light that reveals things for what they are and shows the way.

Jesus and the Law

Despite what his religious opponents thought, Jesus hadn't come to abolish the Old Testament but rather to 'fulfil it'; that is, to bring about everything it promised and pointed to. Not even the tiniest Hebrew letter in it would disappear, he said, until 'everything is accomplished' (Matthew 5:17–18), a reference to his crucifixion. While it looks as if Jesus then went on to do the very opposite – abolish God's Law (5:21–48) – in fact what he challenged wasn't Old Testament teaching but the rabbis' interpretations of it, contrasting what people had heard from them ('You have heard it said') with his own teaching ('But I say to you'), which cut through their hollow sham to a deeper righteousness.

While Jesus, as a good Jew, kept God's Law, for example paying his Temple tax (Matthew 17:24–27), he wasn't afraid to break it where keeping it left people bound rather than free. Hence he didn't hesitate to heal on the Sabbath.

Firm Foundations

The sermon ends with a parable about two builders (Matthew 7:24–27; Luke 6:46–49), underlining the importance of firm foundations for life. In summer the ground would look hard and suitable for building; but when the winter rains came, a house without foundations would quickly collapse. Jesus was claiming to be the foundation stone of what God was building, just as Isaiah had prophesied (Isaiah 28:16).

KEY SAYING

'Blessed are the poor in spirit, for theirs is the kingdom of heaven.'

MATTHEW 5:3

His Teaching: Holiness
BEING DIFFERENT

Jesus' emphasis on God's love shouldn't be misinterpreted as some soft sentiment that let people get away with anything. Like the Old Testament prophets, he combined a strong proclamation of God's love with a strong challenge about God's holiness. The Pharisees had reduced holiness to mere conformity to certain do's and don'ts; but Jesus said real holiness was about what went on inside. Only when that changed could people really be different.

Being Different

'Holy' means 'set apart' or 'different'. The Old Testament sees God as holy because he is *different* from us in every way; Jerusalem was the holy city because the Temple made it *different* from other cities; Israel was holy because it was *different* from other nations.

Jesus' religious contemporaries believed that holiness was crucial to maintaining Israel's identity; but their emphasis on *what* made them different (circumcision, tithing, Sabbath, ritual cleanliness) had become more important than *why* they were meant to be different. Jesus therefore had little time for such externals. For him, holiness wasn't about keeping away from impurity to avoid defilement, but rather going among impurity in order to transform it.

Clean and Unclean

The Old Testament required Israel to treat some things as 'unclean' – things that would defile them, their land or their relationship with God. It included:

- Dietary rules (e.g. no eating pork or blood)
- Morality rules (e.g. no sexual relationships with close family)
- Religious rules (e.g. no mediums or inappropriate sacrifices)
- Practical rules (e.g. no touching lepers or dead animals)

A Jewish *mikvah* (ritual purity bath), used for cleansing before worship.

While some of these are understandable (improperly cooked pork is dangerous, for example), others have no obvious reason other than being part of God's command to 'be holy, because I am holy' (Leviticus 11:45).

Observing these rules was still a normal part of life in New Testament times. However, the scribes and Pharisees had turned laws that were meant to be a delight and a mark of chosenness into an unbearable burden for most people. Jesus said they focused on externals, not realizing that externals can't make people unclean, but only what goes on inside them. '*Nothing outside a man can make him "unclean" by going into him. Rather, it is what comes out of a man that makes him "unclean"... For from within, out of men's hearts, come evil thoughts, sexual immorality, theft, murder, adultery, greed, malice, deceit, lewdness, envy, slander, arrogance and folly. All these evils come from inside and make a man "unclean"'* (Mark 7:15, 21–23).

Social Holiness

Like the Old Testament prophets, Jesus challenged social injustice. However, he rejected militant approaches to achieving this, and in this was a great inspiration to India's pacifist freedom fighter, Gandhi.

Luke, as a doctor, was particularly interested in social matters, highlighting Jesus' teaching on the coming social reversal (Luke 1:52–53; 6:20–26; 16:19–31) and issues of social and economic justice (Luke 3:11–14; 4:18–19; 19:1–10).

Active Holiness

For Jesus, holiness wasn't a list of things to be avoided to keep oneself holy; real holiness was so powerful it engaged with what was unholy and made it holy. That's why, rather than avoiding people and places the rabbis said defiled you, Jesus actively went among them: eating with tax collectors, mingling with prostitutes, talking to Samaritans and Gentiles. Jesus believed true holiness had nothing to fear. In doing this, he was simply doing what God intended for Israel from the beginning. But rather than being 'a light for the Gentiles' (Isaiah 42:6), they had become inward-looking and self-protecting. Jesus himself therefore became that penetrating light, just as Simeon had prophesied over the infant Jesus (Luke 2:29–32).

● SEE ALSO
PHARISEES P. 18
PROSPERITY GOSPEL P. 71
SERMON ON THE MOUNT PP. 46–47

> *The centurion, seeing what had happened, praised God and said, 'Surely this was a righteous man.'*
> LUKE 23:47

WHITEWASHED TOMBS

Pictured are some of the estimated 150,000 tombs on the Mount of Olives overlooking Jerusalem. Pious Jews still seek to be buried here because, according to the Talmud (a compendium of rabbis' discussions and legal opinions), this is where the resurrection of the dead will occur.

Jesus described the Pharisees as 'whitewashed tombs' (Matthew 23:27). Tombs were whitewashed so people wouldn't touch them accidentally, especially at night, and so be defiled. Jesus said that contact with the Pharisees was just as defiling; like tombs, they looked nice on the outside but inside were full of defilement.

RIGHT PRIORITIES

'Woe to you, teachers of the law and Pharisees, you hypocrites! You give a tenth of your spices – mint, dill and cummin. But you have neglected the more important matters of the law – justice, mercy and faithfulness. You should have practised the latter, without neglecting the former. You blind guides! You strain out a gnat but swallow a camel' (Matthew 23:23–24).

Through this ridiculous exaggeration of zealously straining a gnat from their cup while failing to notice the camel in it, Jesus portrays the Pharisees as people whose vision of holiness was over-concerned with minute details while ignoring life's big issues.

Holiness and Money

Jesus taught more about money than prayer – though not 'the prosperity gospel', a recent creation of some branches of middle-class Western Christianity. While Judaism had no problem with wealth (after all, Abraham was wealthy), by Jesus' day poverty was a huge problem, with only a small sector of society being wealthy. Judaism encouraged the rich to give alms to the poor, something Jesus also encouraged (e.g. Matthew 6:2–4). However, he said that wealth could be an enormous hindrance to entering God's kingdom, as one rich ruler discovered when Jesus told him to give it all away (Luke 18:18–29); and the parable of the rich fool (Luke 12:13–21), told to someone wanting Jesus to adjudicate on a family property dispute, underlined the foolishness of an insatiable desire for more.

KEY SAYING

'Blessed are those who hunger and thirst for righteousness, for they will be filled.'

MATTHEW 5:6

His Teaching: The Holy Spirit
GOD'S PERSONAL PRESENCE

Jesus' challenge to people to live holy lives wasn't a call to pull themselves up by their bootstraps, as if somehow they could make themselves more God-like. Jesus said that *holy living* can only come from *the Holy Spirit*, the personal presence of God, whom Jesus said he would send to his followers to replace him when he left this earth. God's personal presence could now always be with us.

Person Not Power

While the Holy Spirit is invisible, Jesus said he isn't a *power* but a *person* – not always easy to grasp when the imagery used of him includes fire, wind and water. But this truth was so important to the New Testament writers that they broke the rules of grammar to make the point. While the Greek word for Spirit (*pneuma*) is neither masculine nor feminine but neuter, they always used a *masculine* pronoun when writing of him – totally incorrect grammatically, but for them totally correct theologically. After all, when Jesus described him as 'another Counsellor' (John 14:16), the word 'another' means 'another of the same kind'. All that Jesus had been to the disciples, the Spirit would continue to be when he returned to his heavenly Father.

The Counsellor

In the Upper Room the Holy Spirit is described as a *paraklētos* (John 14:16, 26; 15:26; 16:7), variously translated 'Counsellor' (New International Version), 'Comforter' (King James Version), 'Helper' (Good News Bible). The word literally means 'someone called alongside', especially to offer help in court (though not in the legal sense of 'lawyer'). That was what Jesus said the Spirit would be: someone coming alongside us to give help when needed.

The translation 'Comforter' is nowadays somewhat misleading, giving the wrong idea; but when the King James Version was published, to comfort meant 'to strengthen' (from the Latin *confortare*). The Holy Spirit is the one who strengthens us in every situation.

Who is the Holy Spirit?

While all four Gospels speak of God's Spirit, John tells us the most about *who* he is. In his conversation with the Samaritan woman (John 4:4–29), Jesus said that *where* we worship is irrelevant; what matters is *how* we do it; and that 'how' is only possible through the Holy Spirit, for the simple reason that 'God is spirit' (4:24); so without the Holy Spirit, how can we possibly find God who is spirit? The Holy Spirit is that aspect of God that helps us connect with him.

In Jesus' teaching in the Upper Room the night before he was crucified, he explained to his disciples some of the Spirit's future roles:

■ Being with believers forever (14:16)

■ Living within God's people so they wouldn't feel like orphans (14:17–18)

■ Teaching Jesus' followers, reminding them of all he said (14:26)

■ Convicting the world of sin, righteousness and judgment (16:8–11)

■ Guiding believers into truth (16:12–13)

■ Glorifying Jesus (16:14)

While a full understanding of the Spirit didn't emerge until after Jesus' death, there are clear indications in his teaching that he was to be everything that Jesus himself was, and therefore no one less than God himself.

RIVERS OF LIVING WATER

'"If anyone is thirsty, let him come to me and drink. Whoever believes in me, as the Scripture has said, streams of living water will flow from within him." By this he meant the Spirit, whom those who believed in him were later to receive' (John 7:37–39).

For the previous seven days at the Feast of Tabernacles, the priests had gone to the Pool of Siloam, taken a jug of water from it and processed back to the Temple where they had poured it out at the altar, remembering how God had provided water for their ancestors in the desert. Now, on the eighth day, 'the last and greatest day' (John 7:37), when there was no water ritual, Jesus challenged worn-out Judaism, saying that in coming to him they would find not just a jug of water but a veritable river flowing from inside them, a river of the Holy Spirit, just like the Old Testament prophets had promised.

'He will baptize you with the Holy Spirit and with fire.'
MATTHEW 3:11

● SEE ALSO
HIS DEPENDENCE PP. 88–89
HIS RELATIONSHIP TO GOD PP. 80–81
TRINITY P. 25

'The wind blows wherever it pleases. You hear its sound, but you cannot tell where it comes from or where it is going. So it is with everyone born of the Spirit' (John 3:8).

The Holy Spirit, and those born of him, is as unpredictable and uncontrollable as the wind.

The Holy Spirit is often depicted as a dove, as in this wall mosaic from the Kykkos Monastery in Cyprus. This is a reference to Jesus' baptism when John the Baptist 'saw heaven being torn open and the Spirit descending on him like a dove' (Mark 1:10).

Blasphemy Against the Holy Spirit

'Everyone who speaks a word against the Son of Man will be forgiven, but anyone who blasphemes against the Holy Spirit will not be forgiven' (Luke 12:10; see also Matthew 12:31–32).

Probably no New Testament passage has troubled Christians more than this, and many have feared that they have committed 'the unforgivable sin' (interpreting that, of course, as whatever their particular sin is). But in context, it's absolutely clear what Jesus meant: the unforgivable sin is the persistent refusal to respond to the Spirit's revelation of who Jesus is. For by doing this, you cut yourself off from the one hope of salvation, just like the Pharisees were doing by ascribing Jesus' work to the devil (Matthew 12:24).

KEY SAYING

'Which of you fathers, if your son asks for a fish, will give him a snake instead? Or if he asks for an egg, will give him a scorpion? If you then, though you are evil, know how to give good gifts to your children, how much more will your Father in heaven give the Holy Spirit to those who ask him!'

LUKE 11:11–13

51

His Teaching: About Himself

GOD WITH US

Many see Jesus as a religious teacher with a simple message: love God, love people. But such a conclusion can only be reached by ignoring much of what Jesus taught, not least about himself. For while his focus was undoubtedly on God and people, it was also on himself. He saw *himself* as the key to God's inbreaking kingdom and a new relationship with God. In many ways, his message was staggeringly egocentric; but the problem he left us was that his actions backed up his claims.

Jesus: The Key to the Kingdom

Many prophets had looked forward to God's coming kingdom, and in Jesus' day many people were eagerly anticipating it. But Jesus gave this expectation a twist by saying that it was *he* who was the key to this kingdom, and that *he* was unlocking the door to it right now. 'If *I* drive out demons by the finger of God, then the kingdom of God has come to you' (Luke 11:20), he replied to some who challenged his miracles, thus inextricably linking God's kingdom to himself and no other.

A Roman house key from Tiberias.

Other Indicators of Jesus' Divinity

He claimed:

■ To have authority to forgive sins (e.g. Mark 2:1–12)

■ To be the bridegroom of the messianic banquet (Mark 2:19)

■ To be Lord of the Sabbath (Mark 1:23–38)

■ To be King David's Lord (Luke 20:41–44)

■ To have the right to cleanse the Temple since it was '*my* house' (Mark 11:15–18)

■ To be involved in the final judgment (Matthew 25:31–46)

While claims alone mean nothing, Jesus reinforced them with a sinless life (John 8:46) and indisputable miracles.

JESUS, THE WAY

'I am the way and the truth and the life. No-one comes to the Father except through me' (John 14:6).
In a multi-faith age it isn't fashionable to claim your religion is the only way; but that's exactly what Jesus did, claiming to be the *only* way to God because of his unique relationship with him.

Did Jesus Claim to be God's Son?

While Jesus rarely spoke overtly about who he was, preferring veiled statements that provoked thinking, his claims are nevertheless clear. For example, in the parable of the tenants (Mark 12:1–12) he spoke of an absentee landlord (of which there were many in his day) who, at harvest time, sent his servants to get his share of the harvest. The tenants beat and even killed successive servants until at last the owner sent his own son thinking they would surely respect him. But they killed him too, wanting to claim the property. The owner therefore had no alternative but to come in person, punishing them and giving the tenancy to others. The religious leaders' reaction to this parable was to look for a reason to arrest Jesus, realizing 'he had spoken the parable against them' (12:12) but failing to see he was claiming to be the Son of God who owned Israel's vineyard.

His final and open claim came at a crazy point: under arrest, on trial for his life. Only now, when the high priest charged him under oath, 'Tell us if you are the Christ, the Son of God', did he reply 'Yes' and described his future coming on the clouds in glory, which proved too much for Caiaphas, who saw such a claim as blasphemy (Matthew 26:62–66).

● SEE ALSO
DID JESUS KNOW HE WAS GOD? P. 25
HIS TITLES PP. 82–85
HIS RELATIONSHIP TO GOD PP. 80–81

And they will call him Immanuel – which means 'God with us'.
MATTHEW **1:23**

The 'I Am' Sayings

John's Gospel contains seven 'I am' sayings, each picking up a key Old Testament idea:

- The bread of life (6:35)

- The light of the world (8:12; 9:5)

- The gate for the sheep (10:7, 9)

- The good shepherd (10:11)

- The resurrection and the life (11:25)

- The way, the truth and the life (14:6)

- The true vine (15:1, 5)

In each of these, Jesus wasn't simply claiming to show us the way or teach us the truth; he was claiming to *be* that way and that truth, to be nothing less than God himself who had been all these things for Israel in the Old Testament.

This astounding claim becomes even stronger when we consider that 'I am' was God's personal name, revealed to Moses at the burning bush (Exodus 3:14). There is a play on words in Hebrew that is lost in translation. When Moses asked God, 'What is your name?', God replied, 'I AM', but then said, 'You can call me HE IS' (*Yahweh*, generally translated in English as 'the LORD' in lower capital letters).

That Jesus was making this claim is clear from people's reactions. In discussing Abraham with the Jewish leaders (John 8:31–59), Jesus claimed, 'Before Abraham was born, I am' (8:58) – no qualification, just 'I am'. The significance wasn't lost on them, for they tried to stone him for blasphemy.

Jesus spoke in a similar way in Gethsemane. When the guards came seeking Jesus of Nazareth, he replied, 'I am [he]'. That more than the obvious was being said is seen in the guards' reaction: 'they drew back and fell to the ground' (John 18:6). It seems that, for that moment, they encountered the divine and it terrified them.

How God's name YHWH (*Yahweh*), 'I AM', appears in Hebrew (reading from right to left).

THE TRUE VINE

Vine cultivation was important in Palestine, and Jesus told several parables about vineyards. The vine's importance is reflected in it being a national emblem of Israel. So when Jesus described himself as 'the true vine' (John 15:1), he was doing nothing less than claiming to be the true Israel.

KEY SAYING

'If you knew the gift of God and who it is that asks you for a drink, you would have asked him and he would have given you living water.'

JOHN 4:10

His Teaching: His Destiny
THE MAN WHO CAME TO DIE

In evil days it's not at all unusual for good people to face tragic endings. History has many such examples, brave men and women who stood up to evil and paid the ultimate price. So was it simply the same with Jesus, his death a mere inevitability for someone who so upset the status quo? At one level, the answer must be yes; but at another, Jesus not only saw what was coming, but prophesied it in amazing detail, even saying that this was the very reason for which he came.

Did Jesus Foresee His Death?

Did Jesus know he would be killed? Some have suggested not, believing that statements about his death in the Gospels were simply the church's later reading-back into the story. But this fails to consider not just Jesus' teaching, but the setting of that teaching. Many people were expecting Messiah, the conqueror of God's enemies and deliverer of God's people; but Jesus interwove this Old Testament theme with another: that of Isaiah's Suffering Servant (Isaiah 52:13 – 53:12) whose *own* death (not the death of God's enemies) would bring salvation, and not just for Israel, but for 'many' (53:11). In putting these two themes together (conquering king and innocent victim), Jesus was saying that the long-awaited deliverance was indeed about to happen, not by force but by suffering; not just for Israel but for 'many'; not just to end Israel's exile but to deal with mankind's root problem, sin. In the light of this, Jesus' predictions of his death are wholly conceivable.

THE SIGN OF JONAH

'A wicked and adulterous generation asks for a miraculous sign! But none will be given it except the sign of the prophet Jonah. For as Jonah was three days and three nights in the belly of a huge fish, so the Son of Man will be three days and three nights in the heart of the earth' (Matthew 12:39–40).

In this reference to an Old Testament story (part of the detail of which are shown in this fifteenth-century painting by Petrus Gilberti), Jesus showed that he expected something as dramatic as Jonah's story to happen to him; something that involved a man who was apparently dead and gone coming back to life again three days later.

Explanations Begin

When Peter at last realized that Jesus was the Christ (or Messiah) and was blessed by Jesus for it (Matthew 16:13–20), he must have felt very pleased with himself. But the feeling was short lived; for 'from that time on' (verse 21) Jesus started to explain to them exactly what sort of Messiah he would be: not a conquering king but a Suffering Servant (verse 21). Jesus foretold how:

- He would suffer many things
- The religious leaders would be involved
- He would be 'killed'
- He would be raised to life on the third day
- It would happen in Jerusalem

Peter's attempt to correct what he saw as Jesus' misunderstanding of what it meant to be Messiah led Jesus to dismiss him as 'Satan' and a stumbling-block (verse 23). Clearly nothing was going to deflect him from the path he knew he had to follow.

● SEE ALSO
CRUCIFIXION P. 102
RESURRECTION PP. 106–107
TRANSFIGURATION PP. 86–87

Getting More Specific

It was on his final journey to Jerusalem that Jesus prophesied with amazing accuracy what would happen to him in a week's time (Matthew 20:17–19). He spoke of:

■ Being betrayed to religious leaders

■ Being condemned to death (i.e. a trial would be involved)

■ The involvement of Gentiles (Romans)

■ Being mocked and flogged

■ His crucifixion

■ Being raised to life on the third day

How Did Jesus Interpret His Death?

For Jesus, his death wasn't simply a demonstration of how much God loved us; he interpreted his death as:

■ **A sacrifice:** At the Last Supper Jesus said, 'This is my blood of the covenant, which is poured out for many for the forgiveness of sins' (Matthew 26:28), a reference to Old Testament sacrifices in which blood was poured out at the altar for forgiveness, showing he saw his death was related to our forgiveness.

■ **A ransom:** As surely as God had ransomed (or redeemed) Israel from slavery in Egypt (Exodus 6:6–8), so Jesus said he would ransom us from sin: 'The Son of Man did not come to be served, but to serve, and to give his life as a ransom for many' (Matthew 20:28).

■ **A victory:** While his crucifixion looked like failure, Jesus saw it as success. His final cry, 'It is finished' (John 19:30), wasn't a cry of despair but one of victory. The Greek expression means 'It's done!', 'It's completed!' or 'It's all paid!' Satan's fall like lightning from heaven (Luke 10:18) was now made secure.

THE TRANSFIGURATION
After his transfiguration (Matthew 17:1–13), depicted in the Russian icon above, Jesus told Peter, James and John not to tell anyone what they had seen 'until the Son of Man has been raised from the dead' (verse 9). Once again he underlined his coming suffering (verse 12) and the betrayal that would lead to his death, though resurrection would follow (verses 22–23).

'Just as Moses lifted up the snake in the desert, so the Son of Man must be lifted up, that everyone who believes in him may have eternal life' (John 3:14–15). In his conversation with Nicodemus, a Jewish religious leader, Jesus referred to this Old Testament story of Moses setting a bronze serpent on a pole when the Israelites were plagued with poisonous snakes. Just as whoever looked to it was healed (Numbers 21:4–9), so Jesus was saying that the goal of his life was to die for others who would 'look' to him and be saved.

KEY SAYING

'The Son of Man did not come to be served, but to serve, and to give his life as a ransom for many.'
MARK 10:45

His Teaching: The New Community
LIFE TOGETHER WITH JESUS

Did Jesus envisage 'the church'? Or was it a later development, established by his followers? Whether he envisaged it in the various forms it has taken over the centuries is probably impossible to answer (though it doesn't take much observation to note that all churches have developed practices that can often seem far removed from how Jesus himself did things). What is clear, however, is that Jesus fully intended to establish a new people, a new Israel, and that any Christianity that is content with merely personal salvation would therefore have found little support from him.

End Time Expectations

There was a general Jewish expectation in Jesus' day that the twelve tribes of Israel would once again be re-assembled before the arrival of the End Time. Jesus' calling of twelve disciples was a deliberate reference to this: he was thereby declaring that he was re-forming Israel, around himself; and that in turn meant the End Time could not now be far away.

The New Israel

While Jesus came fully intending to complete the story begun in the Old Testament, he also gave it a new twist. God was still committed to establishing his people Israel, he said; but that Israel was being reconstituted – around him. *He* was the new Israel, he was the true vine (John 15:1), and all who committed themselves to being his disciples could become part of that new Israel too. It was this new spiritual community, eventually called 'the church', that was now the true embodiment of God's people. And this new community was open to all: men, women, old, young, outcasts, lepers, prostitutes, tax collectors, Jews, Samaritans, non-Jews. There were no religious hoops to be jumped through, no badges of allegiance to be aligned with; simply a willingness to follow Jesus and to learn to do things his way.

After the resurrection, his followers increasingly realized the truth and implications of this. The church came to see that, as the apostle Paul put it, 'there is neither Jew nor Greek, slave nor free, male nor female, for you are all one in Christ Jesus' (Galatians 3:28). This 'new Israel' was at last becoming what old Israel was always meant to be: a people modelling what life is like with God as king and eager to share this good news with others.

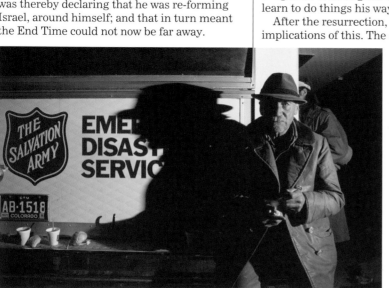

The Salvation Army is one of the best-known expressions of the church in action among the poor and needy as an integral part of the gospel it preaches.

56

The apostles gathered round Jesus...
MARK **6**:30

● SEE ALSO
CHURCH P. 112
DISCIPLESHIP P. 40
WHY TWELVE DISCIPLES? P. 34

Did Jesus Teach About the Church?

The word 'church' (*ekklēsia* in Greek) is actually found only twice in the Gospels, and both examples are in Matthew. In the first (16:18), Jesus promises he will build his church on the rock of Peter and his confession. In the second (18:17), he teaches his followers how to resolve disputes, first by dealing directly with the other party or with another's help if necessary, but if that didn't work, by taking it to the church. So does this lack of reference to 'church' mean that Jesus himself didn't teach about it and that Matthew simply put these words on Jesus' lips from his own later perspective?

Although the actual word 'church' isn't common in the Gospels, the concept certainly is. Indeed the very idea of his central message, the kingdom of God, is impossible without community. Kingship cannot be exercised over one *person*, only over one *people*. It's clear that God's concern throughout the Old Testament had always been for establishing a people, not for saving individuals. It is therefore inconceivable that Jesus would suddenly have abandoned such a fundamental aspect as this, especially when the kingdom lay at the heart of his teaching.

Characteristics of the New Community

The new community that Jesus was building would not be characterized by external badges of belonging like in Judaism, such as circumcision and Sabbath-keeping; rather it would be characterized by attitudes and actions of commitment to one another and others, through things like:

■ Acceptance (e.g. Luke 5:27–32)

■ Forgiveness (e.g. Matthew 18:21–35)

■ Love for one another (e.g. John 13:34–35)

■ Love for enemies (e.g. Luke 6:32–36)

■ Giving to others (e.g. Luke 12:33)

■ Trusting God (e.g. Matthew 6:25–34)

■ Serving one another (e.g. John 13:12–17)

■ Humility (e.g. Matthew 18:1–4)

■ Prayerful dependence on God as Father (e.g. Matthew 6:5–13)

ISRAEL'S OLDEST CHURCH BUILDING

In 2005 this well-preserved mosaic was discovered in the ruins of a rectangular building in the grounds of a prison in Megiddo in northern Israel. Dating from the early third century, the mosaic of two fish (an early Christian symbol) was accompanied by Greek inscriptions saying that the building was dedicated to 'the memory of the Lord Jesus Christ', that it had been paid for by a Roman army officer called Gaianus, and that the communion table was donated by a lady called Ekoptos.

To date, this is the oldest church building ever discovered, just pre-dating the emperor Constantine's conversion. Prior to this Christians had had to meet in secret. The second oldest church building is probably the Church of the Holy Sepulchre in Jerusalem, dating from around AD 330.

Four Core Practices

Luke tells us in his second volume, the book of Acts, that after Jesus' ascension and Pentecost his disciples regularly gathered to do four things: listen to the apostles' teaching, share fellowship, break bread and pray together (Acts 2:42). While these became the characteristic hallmarks of early church gatherings, they were all firmly rooted in the life the disciples had shared with Jesus. They simply continued doing with one another what Jesus had done with them, living a life of community.

KEY SAYING

'Where two or three come together in my name, there am I with them.'
MATTHEW 18:20

His Teaching: God's Judgment
THE BEGINNING OF THE END

While Jesus preached about God's love, he wasn't afraid to also preach about God's judgment. For him, these weren't irreconcilable opposites, but two sides of one coin: love that let us get away with anything wouldn't be true love, and justice that had no love wouldn't be true justice. Both are seen in Jesus' attitude to Jerusalem, loving it, yet prophesying its judgment (Matthew 23:37–38). But what would happen to Jerusalem, Jesus said, was simply a sign of what would happen to everyone who didn't respond to him.

A Day of Reckoning

While Jesus often spoke of his return and a day of reckoning, he said it wouldn't happen yet. We see this, for example, in the parable of the ten minas (coins) (Luke 19:11–27). The master who went away returned, requiring an account from his servants of how they had handled his affairs and rewarding them accordingly. While rewards await the faithful, Jesus said, judgment awaits 'those enemies of mine who did not want me to be a king over them' (19:27).

Looking Ahead

For Jesus, history wasn't going round endlessly in circles but heading towards the End. However, unlike his Jewish contemporaries, he saw that End coming not in one event but in two. In response to his prophecy that the Temple would be destroyed, his disciples asked him *two* questions: 'When will this happen, and what will be the sign of your coming and of the end of the age?' (Matthew 24:3). Failure to separate these two questions and Jesus' answers leads to incorrect views about the future that Jesus saw coming in two stages:

Stage 1: Jerusalem's Destruction (Matthew 24:1–28)

Jesus said difficult times lay ahead in the near future:

■ Many false messiahs would stir Israel to rebellion (verses 4–5).

■ There would be many troubles, described in traditional prophetic imagery (verses 6–8).

■ There would be persecution of his followers, who would by then have spread to other nations (verses 9–14).

■ Jerusalem would be attacked, and 'the abomination that causes desolation' (verse 15) set up in the Temple, but his followers would escape this if they fled Jerusalem (verses 15–22).

■ However, his followers should *not* mistake all this as the End (verses 23–28).

Jesus was warning his followers not to get involved in the coming nationalistic war which would end in catastrophe. Life would continue after it, and so would the gospel, giving everyone a chance to turn to Jesus before God's *final* judgment eventually came.

Stage 2: The Final Days (Matthew 24:29 – 25:46)

Jesus said that '*after* the distress of those days' (24:29) events would happen that would *eventually* lead to the End, marked by his return and God's judgment (24:44 – 25:46):

■ Life would continue as normal (24:37–39).

■ There would be a final battle, described in traditional apocalyptic language (24:29–30).

■ Jesus would return and gather his followers (24:30–31); but since no one, not even he, knew when, we should constantly be ready (24:32 – 25:13).

■ We should make wise use of this interim time (25:14–28), knowing that God's judgment will surely follow for those who reject Jesus (25:31–46).

Romans carry off Jewish spoils in this replica of the Arch of Titus.

'*Jerusalem will be trampled on by the Gentiles until the times of the Gentiles are fulfilled.*'
Luke 21:24

● **SEE ALSO**
ATTITUDES TO THE TEMPLE P. 17
JERUSALEM P. 16
JESUS' RETURN P. 120

The End of the Temple

'*As he was leaving the temple, one of his disciples said to him, "Look, Teacher! What massive stones! What magnificent buildings!" "Do you see all these great buildings?" replied Jesus. "Not one stone here will be left on another; every one will be thrown down"*' (Mark 13:1–2).

For country boys from Galilee, the Temple must have seemed amazing; but Jesus wasn't fooled by its appearance and prophesied its destruction. When the Romans broke through Jerusalem's defences in AD 70 after a four-year war, they ransacked the Temple, setting up their standards in the Holy Place, Daniel's prophesied 'abomination that causes desolation' (Daniel 11:31) referred to by Jesus (Matthew 24:15). Since these bore the emperor's insignia, it sealed the Temple's final desecration. They then set the Temple on fire, its gold adornment melting, seeping into cracks between the huge stones, which the soldiers broke apart to get the gold. This photo shows the Western Wall of the Temple Mount, the only part to survive.

The Temple was now finished with, irrelevant to God's purposes. It had been destroyed, not by the Romans, but by God.

Eternal Destinies

In the parable of the rich man and Lazarus (Luke 16:19–31), Jesus contrasted the destinies of two completely different people: a fabulously wealthy man and a poor man who sat daily outside his gate. Lazarus (the only character ever named in Jesus' parables) died and went to 'Abraham's side', a rabbinic expression for paradise, the home of the righteous awaiting future vindication. The uncaring rich man also died but went to Hades (*not* hell), where Judaism believed the wicked awaited their final judgment. The rich man was in such distress there that he begged Abraham to send Lazarus to give him water (something he had never done for Lazarus). But Abraham said that 'between us and you a great chasm has been fixed, so that those who want to go from here to you cannot, nor can anyone cross over from there to us' (16:27). The rich man begged Abraham to send Lazarus to warn his brothers of their fate, but Abraham said if they hadn't listened to the Scriptures, why would they listen to someone returning from the dead? – an obvious reference to Jesus' own resurrection.

Through this story, Jesus underlined the certainty of a future life, the certainty of both judgment and rewards, and the impossibility of changing things after death. This life is the only chance we have to make our decisions.

KEY SAYING

'*There is a judge for the one who rejects me and does not accept my words.*'
JOHN 12:48

His Miracles: Power Over Sickness
SIGNS OF THE KINGDOM

Even a cursory reading of the Gospels reveals that miracles were a significant part of Jesus' ministry; in fact, almost one-third of Mark concerns miracles. But Jesus' miracles weren't a means of attracting followers, nor even primarily expressions of compassion. They were demonstrations of God's kingdom, showing what happens when God rules. The transformation of the human body was just a picture of the transformation of the human condition that Jesus had come to bring.

Healings of the Blind and Deaf

Many of Jesus' healings concerned the blind and deaf, a picture of the opening of spiritual eyes and ears that he had come to bring. For example, in John's Gospel Jesus heals a man born blind (9:1–12), which immediately leads into debate with the Pharisees. While the miracle was incontrovertible, they were angry he had done it on the Sabbath; so Jesus took the miracle as an opportunity to challenge them about their own spiritual blindness (9:13–41).

The healing of the blind and deaf was very significant to Jews, for Isaiah had prophesied 700 years earlier that this would be a key part of Messiah's work when he came (Isaiah 29:18; 35:5–6). So when John the Baptist, imprisoned by Herod, began to doubt whether Jesus was indeed the Messiah, Jesus told the messengers he had sent, 'Go back and report to John what you hear and see: The blind receive sight, the lame walk, those who have leprosy are cured, the deaf hear, the dead are raised, and the good news is preached to the poor' (Matthew 11:4–5).

MIRACLES AROUND GALILEE

The Gospels record thirty-five specific miracles, as well as referring to lots more. Many of them happened around the Sea of Galilee.

1. CAPERNAUM

■ Freeing a demon-possessed man (Mark 1:21–28)

■ Healing Peter's mother-in-law (Mark 1:29–32)

■ Healing a paralysed man (Mark 2:1–12)

■ Healing a centurion's paralysed servant (Matthew 8:5–13)

■ Raising Jairus's daughter from the dead (Mark 5:21–24, 35–43)

■ Healing a woman with constant bleeding (Mark 6:25–34)

■ Producing a miraculous catch of fish (Luke 5:1–11)

2. CHORAZIN

■ Unspecified miracles, met with unbelief (Matthew 11:20–24)

3. BETHSAIDA

■ Healing a blind man (Mark 8:22–26)

■ Feeding of the 5,000 (Luke 9:10–17)

4. SEA OF GALILEE

■ Walking on water (Matthew 14:22–36)

■ Calming the storm (Matthew 8:23–27)

5. GADARA REGION

■ Freeing a demon-possessed man (Luke 8:26–39)

Miracles and Faith

While miracles and faith are linked, it is important to note the following:

■ Miracles didn't always *depend* on faith. Sometimes people had little faith (John 5:6–7); sometimes they had lots (Matthew 9:21).

■ Miracles didn't always *produce* faith. Ten lepers were healed, but only one came back to say thank you (Luke 17:11–19).

NON-CHRISTIAN WITNESS TO JESUS' MIRACLES

'[Jesus] was a doer of startling deeds…' (Josephus, *Testimonium Flavianum*)

'[Jesus]… practiced sorcery and enticed Israel to apostasy.' (*Jewish Talmud, Sanhedrin, 43a*)

The ruins of Jerusalem's five-porched Pool of Bethesda, where invalids gathered believing that, when the waters were disturbed by its underground spring, the first to climb in would be healed. Here Jesus healed a man who had been paralysed for thirty-eight years (John 5:1–15), time enough for people to know he was truly crippled. Jesus' challenge about whether he wanted to be healed is understandable; his only means of support (begging) was about to be taken away.

The power of the Lord was present for him to heal the sick.
LUKE **5:17**

SEE ALSO
DEMONS P. 91
KINGDOM OF GOD PP. 38–39
POWER OVER NATURE PP. 62–63

Healing with a Difference

What is striking about Jesus' miracles is not so much *what* he did, but *whom* he did it for; because in the eyes of the Jewish religious leaders, he simply healed the wrong sort of people: lepers, outcasts, the unclean, non-Jews. Indeed the kind of healing he did simply isn't found in any contemporary Jewish literature. His opponents' problem was that Jesus healed people who didn't deserve it; but that, of course, was exactly Jesus' point. The healings were pictures of what God is like and concrete demonstrations of his inbreaking kingdom, a foretaste of the hoped-for liberation from spiritual exile.

Rembrandt illustrated Jesus' miraculous acts of healing in his *Christ Healing the Sick*.

CAN MIRACLES HAPPEN?

Some Westerners are sceptical about Jesus' miracles, dismissing them as primitive superstition. But as postmodernism has shown, the scientific worldview isn't the only valid one, and dismissing ancient peoples as fools or frauds because they believed in miracles is unbelievable arrogance. In fact, the vast majority of the world's population today believes in a spiritual dimension and lives accordingly; and many churches still experience healing in Jesus' name.

Were some of Jesus' healings psychological? Possibly, just like any modern doctor's; but that doesn't diminish their reality. However, some cannot have been psychological, such as the healing of a Roman centurion's servant at a distance (Matthew 8:5–13), whom the centurion discovered was healed at the very moment Jesus had prayed.

Methods of Healing

Jesus used a variety of ways of healing people, some straightforward, some more unusual:

■ Laying his hands on people (Mark 6:5)

■ Rebuking sickness (Luke 4:39)

■ Casting out (Matthew 17:18) and rebuking demons (Mark 9:25)

■ Commanding the sick to take action (Mark 2:10–12)

■ Putting mud on eyes (John 9:6) and fingers in ears (Mark 7:33)

While most healings were instantaneous, some at least were gradual (Mark 8:22–25).

Why the Secrecy?

Why did Jesus so often tell people to keep his miracles secret (e.g. Mark 1:43–44), when the more natural thing would be to want everyone to know so he gained more credibility? Jesus didn't want to be misunderstood as a miracle-working Messiah, about to free Israel through demonstrations of miracles and military might. His mission was quite different from that, so he often commanded secrecy (though people tended to ignore him, see Mark 1:45).

His Miracles: Power Over Nature

LORD OVER ALL

If Jesus' miracles had been confined to healings, they might be more easily understandable; after all, they might have been psychological or the result of exceptional medical insight. However, they went way beyond the explainable, breaking nature's rules and power. But then, if what the Gospels believed about this man really was true – that he was no one less than God himself – then none of this is surprising. For if God can't control his creation, who can?

A Byzantine mosaic at Tabgha, commemorating Jesus' feeding of 5,000. The artist was unfamiliar with Galilee's fish as none has two dorsal fins.

FEEDING CROWDS

The Gospels record two stories of Jesus miraculously feeding crowds, one of 5,000, one of 4,000. These aren't variants of the same story, for Jesus referred to them as separate incidents (Matthew 16:8–10). The feeding of 5,000 is the only miracle recorded by all four Gospels (Matthew 14:13–21; Mark 6:30–44; Luke 9:10–17; John 6:1–15); but only John records that the five loaves and two fish came from a little boy (John 6:9), probably his lunch and therefore not substantial. But not only did Jesus feed the crowd from this – 5,000 men plus wives and children (Matthew 14:21) – there was enough left to fill twelve baskets. Since twelve was the number of Israel's tribes, Jesus was thus showing his ability to satisfy all God's people.

The Creator's Creation

Jesus' nature miracles fall into four categories:

■ Controlling it (e.g. calming storms)

■ Stretching it (e.g. feeding 5,000)

■ Ruling it (e.g. walking on water)

■ Conquering it (e.g. raising the dead)

In Jewish thinking, none of this was impossible, for 'nature' wasn't an independent entity but simply the Creator running his universe, usually like clockwork but, when necessary, bending it to his purposes (e.g. Joshua 10:12–13; 2 Kings 20:8–11).

John's Signs

While John knew Jesus had done many miracles, he recorded just seven (John 20:30–31), describing these as 'signs' (e.g. John 2:11) – not mere demonstrations of power, but pointers beyond themselves, like road signs pointing to a destination. Each sign, full of imagery sometimes explained by Jesus, was designed to challenge people and provoke faith. John's seven signs are:

■ Turning water into wine (2:1–11)

■ Healing a royal official's son (4:46–53)

■ Healing an invalid at the Pool of Bethesda (5:1–14)

■ Feeding 5,000 (6:1–15, 25–59)

■ Walking on water (6:16–24)

■ Healing the man born blind (9:1–41)

■ Raising Lazarus (11:1–44)

The 'sign' of the feeding of the 5,000 is illustrated in this painting, *The Miracle of the Loaves and Fishes* by James Tissot.

'*Who is this? Even the wind and the waves obey him!*'
MARK 4:41

● SEE ALSO
HIS RESURRECTION P. 106
'I AM' SAYINGS P. 53
WEDDING AT CANA P. 32

Two Nature Miracles

■ **Calming the storm** (Matthew 8:23–27; Mark 4:36–41; Luke 8:22–25)

Jesus was so exhausted he slept through a storm so bad that it terrified former fishermen. They thought they would drown, but Jesus 'got up, rebuked the wind and said to the waves, "Quiet! Be still!" Then the wind died down and it was completely calm' (Mark 4:39). One can only imagine the disciples' reaction, not least because Jesus rebuked them for not having faith to do this themselves.

■ **Walking on water** (Matthew 14:22–36; Mark 6:45–56; John 6:16–21)

When his disciples were caught on the lake during another storm, Jesus walked across it to join them. Understandably this terrified them, though Peter tried to join Jesus before his faith let him down (Matthew 14:28–30). Jesus' gentle rebuke of his lack of faith (verse 31) suggests he expected him to have been able to do it!

Of course, events like these are impossible; storms don't stop through words, and people can't walk on water. But looking for rational explanations (the storm stopping was a coincidence; Jesus walked on a sandbank) is to miss the point: the *impossibility* of it. *Nobody* could do this kind of thing – unless, of course, he were God; the God who created it in the first place and who was now simply being served by the creation he had made.

Looking through the Arbel Pass towards the Sea of Galilee. The prevailing winds from the south-west rushed through passes like this, causing violent storms to erupt on the lake 'without warning' (Matthew 8:24).

Raising the Dead

■ **The widow of Nain's son** (Luke 7:11–17)

Jesus showed compassion to this widow who had nothing now her only means of support was gone. Turning to her dead son in the open coffin, he told him to get up, which he did. Understandably people were amazed, saying, 'A great prophet has appeared among us' (verse 16), perhaps remembering Elijah's similar miracle (1 Kings 17:8–24). They could come to only one conclusion: 'God has come to help his people.'

■ **Jairus's daughter** (Matthew 9:18–26; Mark 5:21–43; Luke 8:40–56)

The journey to Jairus's house had been interrupted by a woman needing healing, so by the time Jesus arrived, Jairus's daughter was dead. When Jesus told the mourners she wasn't dead but sleeping, they laughed, for they recognized death well enough. So he put them outside and told the girl to get up, which she did. Mark's retention of Jesus'

actual Aramaic words ('*talitha koum*', 'Little girl, get up!') shows how profoundly this event stuck in their memories.

■ **Lazarus** (John 11:1–44)

Although Lazarus was Jesus' friend, when Jesus heard he was sick he deliberately stayed away (verses 3–6). So by the time he arrived, Lazarus had been dead four days (verse 17). This didn't stop Jesus, who declared he was 'the resurrection and the life' (verse 25). He had the stone rolled back and called Lazarus out. Lazarus came back to life and walked out, leaving everyone so shocked, they needed telling to take his grave-clothes off (verse 44).

All three would die again one day, of course; but in the meantime they were powerful signs of Jesus' resurrection and the End Time resurrection of all who believed.

The tomb of Lazarus in Bethany.

KEY SAYING

'*It is I; don't be afraid.*'

JOHN 6:20

His Parables

MYSTERIES EXPLAINED

If Jesus' miracles were his *demonstration* of God's kingdom, then his parables were his *explanation* of it. Through simple stories from everyday life, Jesus revealed profound truths about God's kingdom and how it works. His stories and images had power to reach where other religious teaching couldn't get, scratching where people itched but also provoking where they didn't. Yet behind these simple stories and pictures, sometimes obvious in meaning, sometimes cryptic to draw out faith, lay the mysteries of eternity.

SOME WELL-KNOWN PARABLES

	MATTHEW	MARK	LUKE
Wise and foolish builders	7:24–27		6:47–49
The good Samaritan			10:25–37
The rich fool			12:13–21
The sower	13:1–23	4:1–20	8:4–15
The lost sheep	18:12–14		15:3–7
The prodigal son			15:11–32
The rich man and Lazarus			16:19–31
The unforgiving servant	18:23–35		
The bridesmaids	25:1–13		
The talents	25:14–30		19:11–27
Sheep and goats	25:31–46		

Points About Parables

- They generally have one main point.

- They are generally short, omitting all unnecessary description.

- They are usually based on everyday life, though some use ridiculous exaggeration for impact.

- They can hide as much as they reveal (Mark 4:10–12).

The Power of Story

Rooted as it is in Greek philosophy, Western education is largely based on principles, ideas and theories. For much of the world, however, knowledge is communicated through story-telling; and that was true of the Jews. Much of the Old Testament is story: God revealing eternal truth through a story in history experienced by one nation, with that story itself comprising many other individual stories. So in using stories, Jesus was using a long-practised Jewish method of communicating truth.

One-third of Jesus' teaching was in some sort of parable – a story with a deeper meaning. Parables generally have one key point, and searching for hidden meaning in every detail inevitably leads to missing that point. A parable is rather like a joke; trying to explain it ruins it.

Kingdom Parables

'The kingdom of heaven is like…' is how a cluster of parables in Matthew 13 begins, all underlining that God's kingdom would not come in force as the Jews were expecting, but that it was in fact already here. All of them speak of it having small beginnings, yet destined to triumph. The kingdom is:

- A seed that will grow despite all hindrances (verses 1–23)

- A harvest that is certain despite the weeds trying to choke it (verses 24–30, 36–43)

- A tiny mustard seed (seen here) that becomes the biggest of plants (verses 31–32)

- A small amount of yeast that permeates the batch of dough (verse 33)

- Treasure worth selling everything for (verses 44–46)

- A net catching fish that are sorted at the End (verses 47–50)

● SEE ALSO
'I AM' SAYINGS P. 53
KINGDOM OF GOD PP. 38–39
RIVERS OF LIVING WATER P. 50

The Good Samaritan

The Jerusalem to Jericho road through the Judean wilderness, the setting for the parable of the good Samaritan (Luke 10:25–37), in which a traveller is robbed and left for dead. Ignored by religious people, it is a detested Samaritan who comes to his rescue.

While this parable has sometimes been microanalysed, with each detail given some hidden interpretation, its main point is clear: Jesus had been asked by a religious scholar, 'Who is my neighbour?' The parable's answer, told to people who detested Samaritans, was both simple and shocking: anyone who needs you or will help you. Of course, the parable would have been much more acceptable if it had been about a good Jew helping a Samaritan! But that was a twist that Jesus was not prepared to give it.

Imagery in John

While John's Gospel contains no parables, at least not in the usual sense of that word, his Gospel *is* nevertheless full of imagery, especially from the Old Testament. Some examples include:

■ Vine
Israel was full of vineyards, as Israel's spies had discovered when exploring the land hundreds of years earlier (Numbers 13:17–24). Not surprisingly, therefore, the vine and vineyard became symbols of Israel, with God as its owner (Isaiah 5:1–4). Jesus now claimed to be that new vineyard, 'the true vine' (John 15:1), the true Israel. Only by attachment to him could branches bear fruit (John 15:2–8).

■ Light
Light often symbolized God's presence and goodness in the Old Testament. Jesus now claimed to be that light, not just for Israel, but for everyone. 'I am the light of the world. Whoever follows me will never walk in darkness, but will have the light of life' (John 8:12).

■ Water
Water was an important image of God's provision, refreshing and cleansing, and frequently symbolized his Spirit (Isaiah 44:3; Ezekiel 36:25–27; 47:1–12). Jesus claimed that he was now the provider of that life-giving water. 'If anyone is thirsty, let him come to *me* and drink. Whoever believes in me, as the Scripture has said, streams of living water will flow from within him' (John 7:37–38).

End-Time Parables

Matthew gathers several parables about the End Time:

■ **The faithful and unfaithful servants** (24:45–51): a challenge to be faithful in both our lives and responsibilities.

■ **The wise and foolish bridesmaids** (25:1–13): a challenge to always be ready for Jesus' return.

■ **The talents** (25:14–30): a challenge to use wisely what God has given us, knowing he will require an account one day.

■ **The sheep and goats** (25:31–46): a challenge to live caring lives in the light of the coming judgment.

Other Imagery

Besides full-blown parables, Jesus' teaching was full of all sorts of imagery, normally drawn from everyday life, including:

■ **Birth** (John 3:3–7)

■ **Marriage** (Matthew 25:1–13)

■ **Farming** (John 4:35)

■ **Domestic life** (Matthew 5:13–16)

■ **Nature** (Matthew 6:26–30)

OTHER PARABLES
Other parables cover wide-ranging topics, such as prayer (Luke 18:1–8), self-righteousness (Luke 18:9–14), forgiveness (Matthew 18:21–35) and the dangers of money (Luke 12:13–21).

KEY SAYING
'The knowledge of the secrets of the kingdom of God has been given to you.'
LUKE 8:10

His Authority
WORDS THAT WORKED

Jesus' authority came from neither his knowledge (like the rabbis), nor his achievements (like the Pharisees), nor his role (like the Sadducees), nor his position (like the Romans); it came, quite simply, from who he was. People saw him as 'the real thing', an authentic life, and so were ready to listen to him in a way they wouldn't listen to others.

Authority and His Words

Ask rabbis a question in Jesus' day, and you never got a straight answer. They normally quoted earlier rabbis, often balancing one's teaching against another. But Jesus gave straight answers to straight questions, something that really stood out to people (Matthew 7:28–29). Six times in the Sermon on the Mount he contrasted 'You have heard that it was said' (by the rabbis) with his own 'But I tell you' (Matthew 5:21, 27, 31, 33, 38, 43). In fact, he so believed in his own authority that he could say, 'Heaven and earth will pass away, but my words will never pass away' (Luke 21:33) – words that could have been dismissed as delusions of grandeur had he not had the annoying ability to back up his claims by demonstrations of power. Yet despite these bold claims, he was very aware that his authority wasn't his own, but that it came from his relationship with his heavenly Father (e.g. John 3:34–35; 5:19–23; 17:2).

The religious leaders demanded to know the source of Jesus' authority, but he refused to answer them (Mark 11:27–33), for there were none so blind as those who would not see. Jesus' authority is shown in *The Tribute Money*, the story of which is told in Mark 12:13–17.

Authority and the Sabbath

Jesus' claims to authority came to a head in conflicts over the Sabbath, the Jewish day of rest (Exodus 20:8). For the religious leaders, Sabbath-keeping was a crucial identity marker which they felt Jesus constantly flouted by things like healing the sick (Luke 13:10–17; John 9:13–16) or letting his disciples pick grain (Matthew 12:1–7), all 'work' in their eyes.

But for the most part, Jesus didn't break the Sabbath so much as the many rabbinic rules surrounding it; and it was this challenge to the rabbis' authority that they found so unacceptable. However, there were some occasions when he actually broke Old Testament commandments about the Sabbath, but only when there was genuine need. That's why Jesus healed people on the Sabbath and why, when his disciples were hungry and picked grain ('harvesting', and therefore forbidden), he didn't rebuke them, reminding his critics that even King David had done something similar in time of need (Mark 2:23–28). For Jesus, 'the Sabbath was made for

A Jewish family celebrating the start of Sabbath.

man, not man for the Sabbath' (Mark 2:27).

The many references to Jesus' activity on the Sabbath reflect what a contentious issue this was. But for Jesus, working on the Sabbath was a powerful symbol: if Sabbath rest spoke of remembering God's creation, then his Sabbath miracles spoke of the new creation he had come to bring.

SABBATH PROHIBITIONS

Some of the many activities prohibited by the rabbis on the Sabbath in Jesus' day included:

- Walking more than three-quarters of a mile (1,100 m)

- Rubbing vinegar on a tooth to deal with toothache

- Carrying an object weighing more than a fig

- Applying remedies unless life was endangered

'What is this? A new teaching – and with authority!'
MARK 1:27

● SEE ALSO
'I AM' SAYINGS P. 53
MIRACLES PP. 60–63
PHARISEES P. 18

Authority and Scripture

Jesus fully accepted the Jewish Scriptures as God's word. Hence we find him quoting them often, whether to resist Satan (Matthew 4:1–11), authenticate his actions (Matthew 12:12–13), challenge the self-righteous (Mark 7:1–8), answer questions (Luke 10:25–27) or end debate (Matthew 22:41–46). He believed Scripture's prophecies (Matthew 26:31), accepted its stories (Matthew 12:39–41) and acknowledged its truth, saying that 'not the smallest letter, not the least stroke of a pen, will by any means disappear from the Law until everything is accomplished' (Matthew 5:18) and that 'Scripture cannot be broken' (John 10:35).

His digging beneath religious traditions to get to the heart of what Scripture meant, as in the Sermon on the Mount, often upset people. However, his reinterpretation didn't always make issues easier; sometimes it made them harder, as the disciples discovered when discussing divorce. While acknowledging Moses had permitted divorce, Jesus said God's desire had always been for couples to live together faithfully throughout their lives and that anyone who divorced and remarried, except on the grounds of sexual unfaithfulness, was actually committing adultery (Matthew 19:1–12) – teaching so stark that his disciples thought it better for people to stay single.

The Scroll of Isaiah, from the Dead Sea Scrolls. This was one of the Old Testament books that Jesus quoted most often to back up his teaching.

Delegated Authority

Jesus didn't keep his authority to himself, but delegated it to his disciples, sending them out too to do all he himself had done (Mark 3:14–15; Matthew 28:18–20). This commission included the authority to preach, heal, forgive, teach and do the works he himself had been doing.

The Ultimate Challenge

While human beings have exercised authority in most spheres of life, one where they have never succeeded in doing so is death. Yet the Gospels record three accounts of Jesus raising the dead: Jairus's daughter, the widow of Nain's son, and Lazarus. And at his death on the cross, there was a further outbreak of raisings of dead believers (Matthew 27:51–53), a prophetic anticipation of his own resurrection on Easter Day. This conquest of life's ultimate challenge was one of the most significant expressions of Jesus' authority.

AUTHORITY IN ACTION

Jesus didn't just claim authority, he demonstrated it through such things as:
- Healings
- Exorcisms
- Miracles
- Forgiving sins
- Raising the dead

KEY SAYING

'That you may know that the Son of Man has authority on earth to forgive sins... I tell you, get up, take your mat and go home.'
LUKE 5:24

His Ethics

BEING GOOD, DOING GOOD

Millions have admired Jesus' ethics, even ardent atheist Professor Richard Dawkins describing him as 'one of the great ethical innovators of history'. Jesus' ethics certainly reached new heights, but two things in particular distinguish them: first, he not only taught high ethics, he lived them; second, his ethics were integral to his whole message, thereby preventing us from admiring his ethics while rejecting his teaching about who he was and why he came. For Jesus, *doing* good came out of *being* good.

Examples of Jesus' Ethical Teaching

Of the many ethical issues that Jesus taught about, here are just some examples from Matthew's Gospel:

- Values (5:3–11)
- Anger (5:21–22)
- Forgiveness (5:23–26)
- Revenge (5:38–42)
- Enemies (5:43–48)
- Marriage (5:31–32; 19:1–12)
- Sex (5:27–30)
- Children (18:1–6)
- Speech (5:33–37)
- Giving (6:2–4)
- Materialism (6:19–33)
- Judging others (7:1–5)
- Social responsibilities (22:15–21)

Principles, Not System

Many great teachers have developed coherent ethical systems. That's what the rabbis had done, applying Scripture to the whole of life, creating countless rules for living. But Jesus was different; he had no 'system', just two simple principles:

- Love God with all your being.
- Love your neighbour as yourself.

These two principles, he said, fulfil everything God wants (Matthew 22:36–40). For Jesus, systems and rules could never change a person's ethical behaviour, as the Pharisees proved in his day and communism in our own.

Kingdom Ethics

Jesus' real focus wasn't ethics but eschatology: the belief that the End Times were breaking in *through him*. That's why it's impossible to separate his ethics from his teaching about himself, to follow *them* without first following *him*. His challenge was, 'Come, follow *me*' (Mark 1:17), not 'Come, follow a system'. This alone is when true ethical living begins.

While some have considered Jesus' ethics so idealistic as to be impractical, and therefore only ever intended as interim ethics for the short period they say he envisaged before the End, they are in fact both possible and practical once the decision to follow him is in place.

The Golden Rule

Many religions and philosophies have taught 'the Golden Rule', normally expressed negatively: '*Don't do* to others what you wouldn't want them to do to you'. But Jesus made it utterly positive: '*Do to* others what you would have them do to you' (Matthew 7:12; Luke 6:31). Christian ethics are proactive, not reactive.

'A man who was merely a man and said the sort of things Jesus said would not be a great moral teacher. He would either be a lunatic – on a level with a man who says he is a poached egg – or else he would be the Devil of Hell. You must make your choice. Either this man was, and is, the Son of God; or else a madman or something worse. You can shut Him up for a fool, you can spit at Him and kill Him as a demon; or you can fall at His feet and call Him Lord. But let us not come with any patronising nonsense about His being a great moral teacher. He has not left that open to us. He did not intend to.'
C. S. Lewis

Some said, 'He is a good man.'
JOHN **7:12**

● SEE ALSO
HIS LIFESTYLE PP. 70–71
KINGDOM OF GOD PP. 38–39
SERMON ON THE MOUNT PP. 46–47

Two Key Areas

It's impossible in a book of this length to cover all of Jesus' ethical teaching; but here are two key examples of his radical ethical approach.

1. The Poor

Jesus found great acceptance among the poor and needy, whom he always valued (Matthew 5:3; Mark 12:41–44). He challenged his followers to care for the poor (Matthew 6:2–4; 19:21; Luke 12:33; 14:13–14; John 13:29), something the early church made a priority (Acts 2:45; 4:34–35; 9:36; 24:17; Galatians 2:10). Jesus said that how we care for those in need will be a significant factor at the Last Judgment (Matthew 25:31–46).

2. Pacifism

Jesus renounced all expressions of violence (of which there were many in his day). At a political level, he rejected the popular expectation of a military Messiah who would overcome the Romans, telling his followers rather to overcome through unexpected kindness (Matthew 5:41). At a personal level, he told them not to retaliate but rather to turn the other cheek (Matthew 5:38–39). When Peter tried to defend Jesus at his arrest, cutting off someone's ear in the process, Jesus told him to put away his sword, saying his Father was well able to protect him if that was how he wanted to do things (Matthew 26:47–56; John 18:3–11).

Christians have always been at the forefront of caring for the needy, which has often antagonized atheistic authorities.

Martin Luther King Jr, American civil rights campaigner, was a great believer in Jesus' teaching on non-violence.

Ethical Motivations

Some have seen Jesus' teaching about rewards and punishments as an obstacle to his ethics. After all, acting out of hope of reward or fear of punishment hardly seems the highest ethical motive. In fact, Jesus believed that disinterested goodness (Luke 14:12–14) is the highest motive, and that the reward of simply knowing you have done God's will for which he will one day say, 'Well done, good and faithful servant!' (Matthew 25:23), should be sufficient. But he also said that God rewards right behaviour (Matthew 6:4) and punishes bad or selfish behaviour (Matthew 25:41). He believed that things are judged by their results: 'Every good tree bears good fruit, but a bad tree bears bad fruit' (Matthew 7:17). Good trees are worth keeping; bad ones aren't (7:18–19). So it is with people. Knowing this is how things are, yet not saying so, would surely be the most unethical thing of all.

> **KEY SAYING**
>
> *'Do to others as you would have them do to you.'*
>
> LUKE 6:31

69

His Lifestyle

LIVING LIFE SIMPLY

Visitors to the Third World are often impacted by how little people have there (yet seem happy), while Westerners have so much (yet never seem to be content). Materialism was something that Jesus ruthlessly avoided, not only warning against it, but also deliberately choosing a simple lifestyle for himself – one that left him content and others blessed; a lifestyle that is still a challenge to his followers today.

Simplicity

Jesus lived a simple lifestyle, uncluttered by 'things' and dependent on God. He had no means of transport, having to borrow a donkey when it really mattered (Matthew 21:1–5). He had no home, 'nowhere to lay his head' (Luke 9:58), accepting hospitality wherever it was given. He had no income, receiving support through friends (Luke 8:1–3) and miraculous provision (Matthew 17:27), and encouraging his disciples to trust God when he sent them out (Luke 9:3). Here was a man who believed in simple, faith-filled living.

By contrast, he warned of the dangers of money and materialism (Matthew 6:24; Luke 8:14; 12:13–21; 16:13–14), and some turned away when he challenged their love of wealth (Luke 18:18–30). However, Jesus was no ascetic, avoiding life's pleasures in pursuit of spiritual goals. He could enjoy life, attending meals and weddings, with all the enjoyment they brought. But such things weren't the goal of his life; he could live with them or without them, for his contentment was not in 'things' but in God.

Ruins at Qumran, home to the monastic Essene community. Jesus rejected this sort of lifestyle, preferring engagement with a fallen world rather than retreat from it.

The Amish community in the USA, descended from eighteenth-century immigrants fleeing persecution in Switzerland, live a very simple lifestyle. While some see them as isolated or stuck in the past, they nevertheless present a powerful challenge to Western Christians to consider simpler living.

Community

One of Jesus' first acts was calling twelve disciples, 'that they might *be with him* and that he might send them out' (Mark 3:14). This priority of community wasn't just a convenient mentoring tool; it modelled what the kingdom of God was like, as twelve very different men discovered God's transforming power to enable them to live together. The early church experienced community living (Acts 2:44–45; 4:32–35) – though 'community' didn't mean 'communist': it was voluntary, with no compulsion. Throughout church history, many Christians have practised community living as a testimony to the gospel's power. Sadly, some modern Christianity has developed a huge 'me'-centredness, which is far from Jesus' teaching.

'He went around doing good.'
ACTS 10:38

SEE ALSO
ESSENES P. 18
HIS ETHICS PP. 68–69
THE NEW COMMUNITY PP. 56–57

Singleness

While marriage was the Jewish norm, Jesus chose singleness for the sake of God's kingdom, thereby giving it new dignity. He said that, for some, this was God's calling (Matthew 19:10–12) and therefore it cannot be a 'lower' state. But nor is singleness a 'higher' state. Peter was married (Matthew 8:14; 1 Corinthians 9:5), and Paul anticipated church leaders would be (1 Timothy 3:1–5). In fact, the earliest date for mandatory celibacy for bishops and priests in the Western church wasn't until the Council of Elvira (AD 295–302); and it wasn't until the First Lateran Council (AD 1123) that celibacy was demanded throughout the whole Roman Catholic Church for all clergy. While this is still the position of the Roman Catholic and Eastern Orthodox churches, the Eastern Catholic Church and Protestant churches reject celibacy as essential for priesthood.

'THE PROSPERITY GOSPEL'

This is also known as 'Health and Wealth' or 'Name it and Claim it'. A relatively recent teaching from North America, it is the belief that God wants us to experience material and financial blessing. Biblical support for this is generally drawn from Old Testament promises to Jews, but there seems little to back it up in the teaching or lifestyle of Jesus. Critics see it having more to do with the Western obsession with money and materialism than following the Jesus who had so little he even had to borrow a tomb.

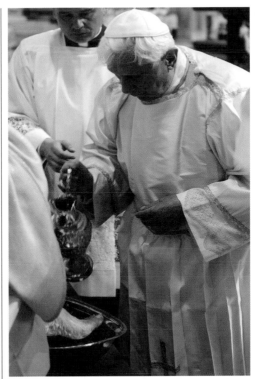

HUMILITY

Here we see the foot-washing ceremony in the Holy Thursday Mass when the Pope washes the feet of twelve priests, commemorating Jesus' washing of his disciples' feet the night before his crucifixion (John 13:1–17). When no servant was available and no one volunteered to do this menial task, Jesus himself did it, not only demonstrating humility, but also modelling it to others. As he said on another occasion, 'Whoever wants to become great among you must be your servant, and whoever wants to be first must be your slave' (Matthew 20:26–27). Humble servanthood should characterize Jesus' followers.

Self-denial

Jesus believed in self-denial, though not as an end in itself. For him, it was about controlling your desires rather than letting them control you (Matthew 5:29–30) and refraining from valid appetites at times to devote yourself to something better (Luke 4:1–13). Like him, his followers had to be ready for the ultimate act of self-denial: 'If anyone would come after me, he must deny himself and take up his cross and follow me' (Matthew 16:24).

The Salvation Army holds annual 'self-denial weeks' when people are encouraged to make sacrifices of money or time to help the poor and needy.

Inclusiveness

In a culture where spiritual, sexual and social segregation created enormous divisions, Jesus mixed with all: religious and non-religious, men and women, adults and children, accepted and marginalized – no one was excluded from his invitation to enter God's kingdom. Such inclusiveness brought him into conflict with the Pharisees, for whom separation, not inclusion, was the key. But from the start of his public ministry in Nazareth, Jesus made it clear, that God's new age of freedom had arrived and that no one was excluded (Luke 4:18–19).

KEY SAYING

'So I tell you, don't worry about everyday life – whether you have enough food, drink, and clothes. Doesn't life consist of more than food and clothing?'

MATTHEW 6:25

His Praying
TALKING TO FATHER

The Jews were very much a praying people, which makes it all the more surprising that Jesus' disciples said, 'Lord, teach us to pray' (Luke 11:1). After all, they had prayed many times: before meals, in the synagogue, at festivals; and yet there was something about *how* Jesus prayed that seemed so different. He made it look so easy, so natural, so enjoyable; and they wanted to know the secret.

Jesus would have often seen the sun rising over the Sea of Galilee as he got up early to pray before the crowds began to gather (Mark 1:35).

The Priority of Prayer

The Gospels are full of instances of Jesus praying. So important was it to him he would do anything to get undisturbed time with his Father, rising early or staying up late (Mark 1:35; 6:36). Even before his crucifixion, his priority was to pray well into the night (Mark 14:32–42). Jesus knew he could do nothing in his own ability, but only through obedience to God's will and dependence on God's Spirit. Prayer was the path to accessing both.

The Hands of the Apostle by Albrecht Dürer (1471–1528), based on the hands of his coal-mining brother Albert. While praying with hands clasped, usually in front of the chest, has become a traditional posture for prayer, it in fact has no biblical basis.

The Simplicity of Prayer

While most religions have sacred places or sacred words for prayer, Jesus had neither. For him prayer was simply *conversation with our heavenly Father*. This has enormous implications for questions about prayer:

■ **Where can we pray? –** *Anywhere!*
For Jesus, where we pray was irrelevant (John 4:20–24). It could be at home (Matthew 6:5–6), in the countryside (Mark 1:35), at favourite spots (Matthew 26:36; John 18:2), in the synagogue (Luke 4:16), in private (Mark 6:46) and in public (John 11:41–42).

■ **When can we pray? –** *Anytime!*
Unlike Judaism, which prescribed prayer twice a day, or Islam, which requires prayer five times a day, Jesus made no demands about when or how often we should pray. He prayed in the morning (Mark 1:35), in the evening (Matthew 14:23), through the night (Luke 6:12), over long periods (Matthew 4:1–2), in crisis moments (Matthew 26:39). His life was full of prayer.

■ **How can we pray? –** *Anyhow!*
Jesus had no special format or vocabulary for prayer. He taught that God is a loving Father who needs no long or fancy words and who knows our needs before we ask (Matthew 6:5–8). There is no technical vocabulary to be learned; we just need our ordinary language, as Jesus himself showed.

■ **What can we pray? –** *Anything!*
For Jesus, prayer wasn't just about lofty spiritual matters, but also down-to-earth things, like daily needs and concerns (Matthew 6:11, 25–34) and protection (Matthew 6:13; John 17:11–15).

'Lord, teach us to pray.'
LUKE 11:1

● SEE ALSO
ABBA P. 36
JEWISH PRAYER P. 28
PRAYER-SHAWLS P. 18

The Lord's Prayer

The best-known Christian prayer is the Lord's Prayer, recorded by Matthew and Luke in slightly different forms:

MATTHEW 6:9–13	LUKE 11:2–4
Our Father in heaven,	Father,
hallowed be your name,	hallowed be your name,
your kingdom come,	your kingdom come.
your will be done	
on earth as it is in heaven.	
Give us today our daily bread.	Give us each day our daily bread.
Forgive us our debts,	Forgive us our sins,
as we also have forgiven our debtors.	for we also forgive everyone who sins against us.
And lead us not into temptation,	And lead us not into temptation.
but deliver us from the evil one.	

The differences in the two versions perhaps reflect different occasions when Jesus taught it; but they are minor, either unpacking the same idea (the kingdom coming is about God's will being done) or Jewish wording rather than Gentile (Matthew describing sins in the traditional Jewish language of a debt to God).

While Matthew's version is *a pattern* ('This then is *how* you should pray'), Luke's is *a prayer* ('When you pray, *say...*'). Both approaches have been followed by Christians. Jesus' warning about mindless repetition when praying (Matthew 6:5–8) means that Christians should not let this prayer become mere religious ritual, however.

The prayer falls into two sections:

■ **Prayer about God:** the honouring of his name, the coming of his kingdom, and the doing of his will. Starting with God keeps things in perspective.

■ **Prayer about us:** prayer for present need, past sin and future welfare; no aspect of life is excluded.

With such a model for prayer, Martin Luther says, 'no one can excuse himself by saying he doesn't know how to pray or what to pray for'.

Keeping Going

'Why didn't God answer my prayer?' is a question many have asked. The Bible shows it is sometimes because God knows more than we do, or because things need to fit into a bigger plan, or because he is dealing with our character. Nevertheless Jesus encouraged his disciples 'that they should always pray and not give up' (Luke 18:1), going on to tell the parable of the persistent widow (18:2–8) who eventually got what she needed because she kept going.

The Father Who Hears

Jesus taught that God is not some remote deity, but rather our heavenly Father, our *Abba* ('daddy' in Aramaic) who hears us (Matthew 6:6). While Islam has ninety-nine names for God, 'Father' isn't one of them, being seen as too familiar; but for Jesus, this summed up the heart of the relationship we can have with God through him.

Praying with raised hands is particularly common among Pentecostal or charismatic Christians, but is also practised by clergy in more traditional churches at certain points in services. In many ways, this is a more biblical posture for prayer than bowing heads or clasping hands (e.g. Nehemiah 8:6; Psalm 28:2; Luke 24:50; 1 Timothy 2:8).

KEY SAYING

'When you pray, say: "Father..."'
LUKE 11:2

His Attitude to Religion
NEW WINE, NEW WINESKINS

Jesus wasn't anti-Jewish; after all, he was himself a Jew and grew up believing Judaism's truths and following its traditions. What he was opposed to was what the religious leaders had turned Judaism into: an old, worn-out wineskin, not flexible enough to contain the new thing God was doing (Mark 2:18–22). New wine needed new wineskins; the old religious wineskins, no longer fit for purpose, had to go. It was time for new beginnings.

Religious Authorities

Jesus often found himself in conflict with the religious authorities, not because he set out to – indeed he was as happy to spend time with them as he was others (e.g. Luke 11:37); it was simply that they wanted to maintain what he wanted to replace. Clashes occurred for different reasons:

■ **The rabbis** were angered by his rejection of their traditional interpretations of the Law; but for Jesus, these kept people from God (e.g. Matthew 5:21–48), even taking precedence over God's word (Mark 7:8).

■ **The Pharisees** were angered by his refusal to uphold traditional identity markers like Sabbath-keeping (Mark 2:23–24) and ritual purity (Luke 11:38); but for Jesus, such externals blinded them to deeper issues (Matthew 23:23–24), and he warned people of their hypocrisy (Luke 12:1).

■ **The Sadducees** were worried Jesus might upset the status quo, causing Rome to clamp down heavily and leading to their influence being lost; but for Jesus, their ignorance of Scripture (Matthew 22:23–32) was as dangerous as their politics, and he warned people to beware of them too (Matthew 16:6).

Religious Practices

One thing that angered Jesus was how the scribes and Pharisees focused so much on externals, often to the exclusion of what those externals pointed to, and sometimes even helping them avoid responsibilities (Mark 7:9–13). For them, these externals were identity markers that must be kept if God were to redeem Israel, but for Jesus they were just empty shells that had once housed life but did so no longer. They included:

■ **Fasting:** while Jesus himself fasted (Matthew 4:1–2) and taught his followers to do so (Matthew 6:16–18), he refused to comply with requirements of twice-weekly fasts as a mark of spirituality.

■ **Tithing:** while there are no references to Jesus tithing, it seems likely that, as a Jew, he would have done so, especially since he encouraged others to (Matthew 23:23). He certainly encouraged generous, discreet giving (Matthew 6:2–4) and commended a widow's

sacrificial giving (Mark 12:41–44).

■ **Praying:** while Jesus prayed often, he challenged those who prayed for show (Matthew 5:5-8; Luke 18:9-14).

■ **Ritual washings:** Jesus had little time for the ritual washings that Judaism had developed. He was more concerned with the inside of a person than the outside (Matthew 15:1–20; Luke 11:37–41).

■ **Sabbath:** Jesus wouldn't comply with their nit-picking additional rules about the Sabbath which added more than God had ever intended (e.g. Matthew 12:1–14; John 5:1–30).

Obsession with all these rules led them to 'strain out a gnat but swallow a camel' (Matthew 23:24).

● SEE ALSO
HIS AUTHORITY PP. 66–67
JERUSALEM P. 16
PHARISEES P. 18

'If we let him go on like this, everyone will believe in him, and then the Romans will come and take away both our place and our nation.'

JOHN 11:48

PARABLE OF THE PHARISEE AND TAX COLLECTOR

In this parable (Luke 18:9–14) Jesus contrasted the self-righteous Pharisee, so confident of his achievements he wanted everyone to know about them (verses 9, 11), with the humble and repentant tax collector who begged for mercy (verse 13). 'I tell you that this man, rather than the other, went home justified before God. For everyone who exalts himself will be humbled, and he who humbles himself will be exalted' (verse 14).

THE TEMPLE

What troubled Jesus about the Temple was what it had come to represent. Its physical domination was a picture of its crushing spiritual domination, symbolizing all that was wrong with Israel, and therefore it would very soon be torn down, Jesus said.

Conflicts with Pharisees

Right at the beginning of his Gospel, Mark shows how quickly the Pharisees became upset with Jesus.

Hypocrisy

Shown here is a theatrical mask from ancient Greece, like those that would have been used in theatres in Greek cities like Sepphoris. The Greek for 'actor' is *hypokritēs*, from which the word 'hypocrite' comes: someone playing a part or pretending to be something they are not. Jesus ruthlessly exposed the hypocrisy of religious leaders (Matthew 6:1–18; 23:13–33), challenging them for saying one thing but doing another, and for placing unrealistic burdens on people. Matthew's Gospel in particular underlines the dangers of hypocrisy.

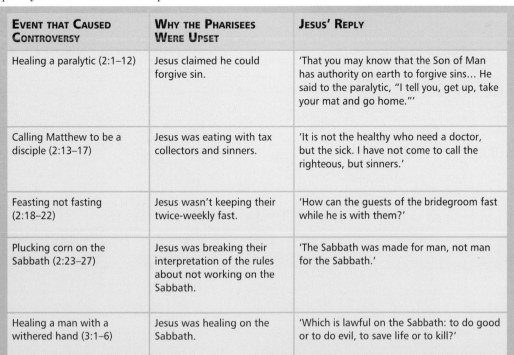

EVENT THAT CAUSED CONTROVERSY	WHY THE PHARISEES WERE UPSET	JESUS' REPLY
Healing a paralytic (2:1–12)	Jesus claimed he could forgive sin.	'That you may know that the Son of Man has authority on earth to forgive sins… He said to the paralytic, "I tell you, get up, take your mat and go home."'
Calling Matthew to be a disciple (2:13–17)	Jesus was eating with tax collectors and sinners.	'It is not the healthy who need a doctor, but the sick. I have not come to call the righteous, but sinners.'
Feasting not fasting (2:18–22)	Jesus wasn't keeping their twice-weekly fast.	'How can the guests of the bridegroom fast while he is with them?'
Plucking corn on the Sabbath (2:23–27)	Jesus was breaking their interpretation of the rules about not working on the Sabbath.	'The Sabbath was made for man, not man for the Sabbath.'
Healing a man with a withered hand (3:1–6)	Jesus was healing on the Sabbath.	'Which is lawful on the Sabbath: to do good or to do evil, to save life or to kill?'

KEY SAYING

'No-one pours new wine into old wineskins. If he does, the wine will burst the skins, and both the wine and the wineskins will be ruined. No, he pours new wine into new wineskins.'

MARK 2:22

His Attitude to People

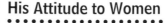

EVERYBODY WELCOME!

Not once do we find Jesus hesitating to do something because of what others might think. That's why we find him mixing with people he shouldn't have mixed with in places he shouldn't have gone to, at least as far as the religious leaders were concerned. But for those for whom he crossed these boundaries, his attitude was the kindest thing they had ever experienced.

His Attitude to Women

Women were often seen as little more than possessions, useful as wives and mothers but responsible for most (if not all) temptation and sin. But Jesus' attitude was so radically different, cutting through traditional values and accepting women on a par with men, regardless of their social or marital status. So we find him:

■ Having women disciples (Luke 8:1–3) and teaching them alongside men (Matthew 14:21; Luke 10:38–42), even though most rabbis discouraged women from studying the Scriptures

■ Mixing freely with women, especially those seen as outcasts because of their lifestyle (Luke 7:36–50), origins (Mark 7:24–30) or morality (John 4:4–26)

■ Refusing to pin the blame on them for sexual misconduct, like men usually did (John 8:1–11)

■ Not seeing them as unclean during menstruation (Mark 5:25–34)

■ Using images and stories relevant to them (Luke 4:24–26; 5:36; 13:20–21; 15:8–10; 18:1–8)

■ Affirming their equality at the resurrection (Luke 20:27–38)

■ Ensuring they were the first to witness the resurrection, even though a woman's testimony was dismissed by Judaism (Matthew 28:1–8)

It is highly likely that Christianity was so attractive to women because of the equal status it afforded them.

CONTEMPORARY ATTITUDES TO WOMEN

■ 'A woman is inferior to her husband in all things.' (Josephus, first-century AD Jewish historian)

■ 'Women are best suited to the indoor life which never strays from the house.' (Philo, first-century Alexandrian Jewish philosopher)

■ 'Blessed art Thou, O Lord our God, King of the universe, who hast not made me a woman.' (One of the eighteen benediction prayers prayed by Jewish men three times a day)

His Attitude to Children

While Jews saw children as God's blessing, they were nevertheless the least important members of the community. But Jesus welcomed children, stressing the importance of receiving them with kindness, as though receiving him (Mark 9:36–37), and giving severe warnings about those who harmed them (Matthew 18:6). He even rebuked his disciples for trying to keep children away from him (Mark 10:13–16) and used them as examples of the trust and humility needed in God's kingdom (Matthew 18:1–4).

● SEE ALSO
SAMARITAN WOMAN P. 32
THE POOR P. 69
ZACCHAEUS P. 42

To all who received him, to those who believed in his name, he gave the right to become children of God.

JOHN 1:12

The Human Condition

While Jesus was always kind towards people, he wasn't blind to what they were like nor excusing of their behaviour. He had a profound ability to both demonstrate God's love, yet also help people see what they were really like. He used a variety of language to portray their condition without God, describing them as:

■ **Blind** (Matthew 15:14; John 9:13–41): but Jesus said he had come to bring 'recovery of sight to the blind' (Luke 4:18).

■ **Hungry** (Matthew 5:6): but Jesus said, 'I am the bread of life. He who comes to me will never go hungry' (John 6:35).

■ **Thirsty** (John 4:15): but Jesus said, 'If anyone is thirsty, let him come to me and drink. Whoever believes in me, as the Scripture has said, streams of living water will flow from within him' (John 7:37–38).

■ **Weary** (Matthew 11:28): but Jesus said, 'Come to me, all you who are weary and burdened, and I will give you rest' (Matthew 11:28).

■ **Lost** (Luke 15:1–32): but Jesus said, 'The Son of Man came to seek and to save what was lost' (Luke 19:10).

■ **Dead** (Matthew 23:27: Luke 9:60); but Jesus said, 'I have come that they may have life, and have it to the full' (John 10:10).

Yet Jesus' insights didn't lead him to highlight people's failure or sin; he did that very rarely, knowing that most people realize their failings without being told, and that what they need is help in unravelling the mess and making things right again; and that's what Jesus focused on. While his religious contemporaries merely laid ever-increasing burdens on ever-more wearied people that highlighted how bad they were, Jesus always gave people hope.

Jesus heals a deaf mute in this 1635 painting by Batholomeus Breenbergh.

EATING TOGETHER

Sharing meals was (and is) a central part of Middle Eastern culture, demonstrating hospitality, acceptance and friendship. However, eating together was riddled with social and religious boundaries, with status and hierarchy, which is why Jesus' parable of the wedding banquet was so shocking (Luke 14:15–24). But Jesus didn't just teach radical inclusion, he practised it (Matthew 9:10), trampling on issues of exclusivity and status by eating with people of all kinds, backgrounds and status. For him, all were welcome in God's kingdom.

His Attitude to the Marginalized

One of the most striking aspects of Jesus' ministry is how he welcomed those that society saw as outcasts, whether for spiritual or cultural reasons. These marginalized included:

■ **Lepers** (Matthew 8:1–4; 11:1–4; 26:6), whose contagious disease led to them being seen as unclean and therefore isolated.

■ **Tax collectors** (Luke 5:27–32; 15:1–7), who were so despised as collaborators that rabbinic literature permitted you to lie to them. Jesus took people's hostility towards Zacchaeus and drew it upon himself (Luke 19:1–10).

■ **Sinners** (Luke 7:36–50), by which religious people meant the sexually immoral.

■ **The unclean**, who didn't keep religious rituals such as ritually washing before meals (Mark 7:1–23).

■ **Non-Jews**, rejected by others but accepted by him (Matthew 8:5–13; Mark 7:24–30).

Jesus' attitude to all these was one of love and acceptance, no strings attached.

KEY SAYING

'The Son of Man came to seek and to save what was lost.'

LUKE 19:10

His Audience
RESPONSES TO JESUS

Not surprisingly, Jesus' ministry was mainly to Jews; after all, he lived in Palestine (where most people were Jewish) and seldom set foot outside it. One might perhaps have expected, therefore, that his own people, eagerly awaiting the arrival of Messiah, would have provided a good audience for him; but in fact, his reception among them was mixed, and it was sometimes better among the Gentiles, proving that 'only in his home town and in his own house is a prophet without honour' (Matthew 13:57).

Nazareth, Jesus' home town, the first place to reject him.

His Mission to Jews

Jesus found a varied reception among his own people, for Israel at this time was far from being a unified community, with many diverse social and religious groupings who responded to him in different ways:

■ Ordinary people

Often described simply as 'the crowd', ordinary people received Jesus well. His lively teaching, backed up by miracles, made them listen in a way that the rabbis' traditional teaching didn't. They were 'amazed at his teaching' (Matthew 7:28), 'listened to him with delight' (Mark 12:37), and said, 'We have never seen anything like this!' (Mark 2:12). Such was his impact that the Pharisees complained, 'The whole world has gone after him' (John 12:19), though the reality was that opinions were often divided over him (John 7:12–13, 40–43), and at the end everybody was ready to abandon him.

■ 'Sinners'

Often linked with 'tax collectors', 'sinners' was the general disparaging term the scribes and Pharisees used for anyone outside their group – those they considered 'outside' Israel, either because they collaborated with Gentiles (like the tax collectors), or failed to observe Jewish rituals, or lived overtly sinful lives (like prostitutes). Yet these were the people Jesus loved to spend time with, earning him the title 'friend of sinners' (Luke 7:34). This group was always ready to welcome Jesus (Matthew 9:10), no doubt because of his readiness to accept them as they were.

■ Religious leaders

It was among the religious leaders – the Sadducees (the priestly families that ran the Temple), scribes (the copiers and teachers of the Law) and Pharisees (those who sought to rigorously apply that Law in everyday life) – that Jesus found his most unreceptive audience. They were fiercely protective of their knowledge and traditions; so Jesus' teaching constantly cut across them, producing strong reactions (Luke 5:21; 7:39; 16:14; John 7:32) and ultimately leading to them plotting his death (Matthew 12:14; 21:43; John 11:45–57). However, while some Pharisees were always trying to catch Jesus out (Matthew 22:15; John 8:6), others, like Nicodemus, wanted to give him a fair hearing (John 3:1–2).

■ His town and family

While his home town of Nazareth initially welcomed Jesus when he returned (Luke 4:14–15), their reaction soon changed to anger when he suggested that God had a place for the Gentiles in his kingdom (Luke 4:24–30), and he had to relocate to Capernaum as his base. His own family's reaction was little better, at least initially. While his mother Mary stood by him to the end (Joseph had probably died when he was young), even she was worried by the intensity of his ministry and came to Capernaum with Jesus' brothers 'to take charge of him, for they said, "He is out of his mind"' (Mark 3:21). John notes, later in Jesus' ministry, that 'even his own brothers did not believe in him' (John 7:5). This rejection by his family must have been difficult for Jesus to bear.

The common people heard him gladly.
MARK **12:37**

● SEE ALSO
HIS NATION PP. 16–17
HIS PEOPLE PP. 18–19
NICODEMUS P. 43

40 km
30 miles

SYRIA

PHOENICIA

Sidon●

▲Mt Hermon

2
Tyre●

4
● Caesarea Philippi

GAULANITIS

1 7
Capernaum●
Sea of
Galilee
GALILEE
Tiberias●

3
DECAPOLIS

esarea●

5
SAMARIA
Sebaste●

Jordan

6
PEREA

ISRAEL

8
Jerusalem●

JUDEA   Dead
Sea

His Mission to Gentiles

1. 'Many people came to him from Judea, Jerusalem, Idumea, and the regions across the Jordan and around Tyre and Sidon' (Mark 3:8). Even early in his ministry, Jesus' reputation spread beyond Galilee, attracting people from surrounding nations.

2. It was in the Phoenician town of Tyre, a strongly Hellenistic city, that Jesus healed the daughter of a Gentile woman, commending her for her faith (Mark 7:24–30).

3. In the Decapolis, a league of ten Greek cities, Jesus healed a deaf and mute man (Mark 7:31–37).

4. Jesus visited villages around Caesarea Philippi (Mark 8:27), a centre of worship to the Greek god Pan. This was almost entirely a Gentile area, but it was here that Jesus began to reveal to his disciples who he really was (Mark 8:27 – 9:1) and on nearby Mount Hermon that he was transfigured (Mark 9:2–13).

5. Hostilities between Jews and Samaritans were both deeply felt and long-standing, going back to events some five centuries earlier. But Jesus refused to maintain these ancient differences. After his encounter with the Samaritan woman he gladly taught in Samaria (John 4:39–42). He also healed a Samaritan leper (Luke 17:11–19) and preached wherever he was accepted (Luke 9:51–56).

6. While never mentioned by name, Jesus ministered in Perea, referred to simply as 'the other side of the Jordan' (Matthew 19:1), where he preached and healed in this mixed Jewish–Gentile community (19:2).

7. A Roman centurion drew admiration from Jesus for his faith which led to the healing of his servant (Luke 7:1–10). Not even the Gentile Roman oppressors lay beyond Jesus' compassion.

8. After his resurrection, Jesus told his disciples to preach his message 'to all nations, beginning at Jerusalem' (Luke 24:47; see also Matthew 28:18–20; Acts 1:8) For the church to have become a worldwide movement from such insignificant beginnings shows that missionary seeds must have been sown in the disciples by Jesus himself, or otherwise they would have remained a minor Jewish sect.

Remains of the Temple of Sebaste (Greek for 'Augustus') on the acropolis of Samaria, built by Herod the Great, symbolizing the pagan nature of Samaria at this time. Yet many Samaritans believed in Jesus.

KEY SAYING

'Whoever hears my word and believes him who sent me has eternal life.'

JOHN 5:24

79

His Relationship to God
THE FATHER'S SON

Even before he set foot in this world, it was clear that Jesus was going to be no ordinary person. Angels said he would be a king and the Son of the Most High (Luke 1:32–33) and would be called Immanuel, 'God with us' (Matthew 1:23). Even his conception was miraculous (Matthew 1:18; Luke 1:34–35). Clearly this was someone special. But how special did Jesus himself think he was? The Gospels provide a startling answer.

HIS PRAYING

Jesus was profoundly dependent on prayer, doing whatever he needed to get undisturbed time with his heavenly Father (e.g. Mark 1:35). His prayers show an intimacy not found anywhere else in Jewish literature, especially his calling God *Abba* ('daddy'), something quite unparalleled in Judaism. His longest prayer in John 17 shows a special intimacy between him and his Father.

Christ Going Out Alone into a Mountain to Pray, by James Tissot.

A Special Relationship

It's clear that Jesus was aware of a special relationship with God from an early age. When his parents, anxious they had lost their twelve-year-old son, found him talking with rabbis in the Temple, his reply was simply, 'Didn't you know I had to be in my Father's house?' (Luke 2:49) – something no right-thinking Jew would ever have claimed, that God was their Father. But as his ministry began, it became clear he was claiming a relationship with God that wasn't just special but unique, something his opponents were quick to condemn him for. 'For this reason the Jews tried all the harder to kill him... he was even calling God his own Father, making himself equal with God' (John 5:18).

Veiled Claims

While Jesus never openly stood up and shouted, 'I am God!', he made veiled yet unmistakable claims of a unique relationship with God. These included:

■ **His miracles:** not just works of power or compassion but a demonstration of the freedom that only God's Spirit can bring (Luke 4:18–19).

■ **His words:** not just words of yet another teacher, but words that fulfilled the Jewish Law (Matthew 5:17) and that 'will never pass away' (Matthew 24:35). He even claimed that our response to his words would determine our eternal destiny (Mark 8:38).

■ **His forgiveness:** claiming the right to forgive people's sins, something any Jew knew God alone could do. So the religious leaders rightly asked, 'Who is this fellow who speaks blasphemy? Who can forgive sins but God alone?' (Luke 5:21). But to prove his authority to forgive, he went on to heal the man he had forgiven.

■ **His actions:** riding into Jerusalem on a donkey, deliberately fulfilling messianic prophecy (Matthew 12:1–11; Zechariah 9:9) and then cleansing the Temple, another messianic act (Matthew 21:12–16).

■ **His titles:** using names and titles that show an unmistakable awareness of a unique relationship with God.

■ **His acceptance of people's acknowledgment** – blessing Peter when he grasped who Jesus was and said, 'You are the Christ, the Son of the living God' (Matthew 16:16) and letting Thomas call him, 'My Lord and my God!' (John 20:28).

Alone, these might be explained away, but together they form a powerful picture of who Jesus was claiming to be and his relationship with God.

'*You, a mere man, claim to be God.*'
JOHN **10:33**

● SEE ALSO
HIS ORIGINS PP. 24–25
HIS TEACHING ABOUT HIMSELF PP. 52–53
HIS TITLES PP. 82–85

THE GLORY OF GOD

'We have seen his glory, the glory of the One and Only, who came from the Father, full of grace and truth' (John 1:14). John used the word 'glory' or 'glorify' forty-one times. In the Old Testament God alone was the source and object of glory, but John wanted us to know that in Jesus that same glorious God had come among us.

Early Church Reflections

Within a short time after his death, the early church was making amazing claims about Jesus, often at the cost of his followers' lives:

■ John

'In the beginning was the Word, and the Word was with God, and the Word was God... The Word became flesh and made his dwelling among us' (John 1:1,14).

■ Paul

'Christ Jesus, being in very nature God, did not consider equality with God something to be grasped, but made himself nothing... he humbled himself and became obedient to death... Therefore God exalted him to the highest place... that at the name of Jesus every knee should bow... and every tongue confess that Jesus Christ is Lord' (Philippians 2:5–11).

'He is the image of the invisible God... by him all things were created... and in him all things hold together... For God was pleased to have all his fullness dwell in him' (Colossians 1:15–19).

■ The author of Hebrews

'The Son is the radiance of God's glory and the exact representation of his being, sustaining all things by his powerful word' (Hebrews 1:3).

What clinched things for them was the resurrection, convincing them that the man who had lived among them was no one less than God himself. But where would that idea have come from if not from Jesus himself?

Amen!

We normally use 'Amen' at the end of prayers; however, Jesus didn't put it at the end but at the beginning. We miss that because modern translations use phrases like 'I tell you the truth', but 'Amen' actually occurs 100 times in the Greek texts of the Gospels. Originally used in the Old Testament as a personal or congregational response to another's prayer, it was a way of affirming your agreement or asserting the truth of what had been said. But Jesus affirmed the truth of what he said even before he said it. By making it the first word of his saying, he was not only emphasizing the importance of what he said but also its truth. No other example of its use in this way has ever been found in Jewish writings, reflecting Jesus' perception of his unique authority as God's unique messenger.

KEY SAYING

'*I and the Father are one.*'
JOHN 10:30

His Titles: The Human Aspect
SON YET SERVANT

While none of us has any say about the name we get at birth, the names and titles we acquire during life say a lot about us; and the same was true for Jesus. The titles he adopted for himself, or accepted from others, all add to our understanding of who he thought he was; and the inevitable conclusion this leads to puts him in a different category from any other religious leader.

Christ in Glory with St Martin, St Stephen, and St John the Baptist by Pomponio Amalteo, 1549.

SON OF DAVID

Although rarely used today, this title was important to Jesus' original hearers, who were expecting a descendant of King David (seen here in Michelangelo's statue) to become Israel's king one day and through whom all the promises to David would be fulfilled. That's why the Gospels make clear that Jesus was indeed a descendant of David through recording his genealogy (Matthew 1; Luke 3). Although people sometimes used this title of Jesus (Mark 10:47), he generally avoided it because of its nationalistic overtones.

Son of Man

Even a cursory reading of the Gospels reveals that this was Jesus' favourite title, used only by himself and created for himself, though not from scratch. It had an Old Testament background: Psalm 8, where it describes humankind in its lowliness, and Daniel 7:13–14, where it describes a glorious heavenly figure receiving an everlasting kingdom, worshipped by all nations. These two ideas summed up exactly who Jesus claimed to be: a glorious heavenly being, ruling everything and worthy of worship, yet who became a humble human being through the incarnation. By putting these two apparently conflicting ideas together, Jesus maintained a certain mystique that demanded further thinking and faith.

The title eventually fell out of common use, probably because its meaning wasn't obvious as the gospel spread beyond Israel into the Gentile world.

THE NAZARENE

'You also were with that Nazarene, Jesus,' the servant said to Peter (Mark 14:66), reflecting the contempt in which a 'Nazarene' (someone from Nazareth) was held (e.g. John 1:46). The first Christians were sometimes called Nazarenes (Acts 24:5), so its use may well go back to Jesus himself.

The modern-day Church of the Nazarene is an international evangelical church with roots in the nineteenth-century Holiness movement. A more superstitious use of the term is found in *The Black Nazarene* seen here: a 200-year-old wooden sculpture of Christ considered to have miraculous powers by its Filipino devotees which is paraded in a twice-yearly procession, the largest in Manila.

● SEE ALSO
HIS TEACHING ABOUT HIMSELF PP. 52–53
HIS TITLES PP. 82–85
INCARNATION P.124

...[Jesus] made himself nothing, taking the very nature of a servant, being made in human likeness.
PHILIPPIANS 2:7

Messiah

This is the title Christians use most frequently of Jesus today, though in a form they don't normally recognize. The Hebrew word *mašiah* ('anointed one') was rooted in the Old Testament practice of anointing priests and kings for God's work. While Israel therefore had had many 'anointed ones', a growing belief developed that God would one day send an ultimate 'anointed one' to deliver his people: 'the Messiah', or in Greek, *Christos*. So when Christians call Jesus 'Christ' they're in fact saying 'Jesus the Messiah', the man God anointed to deliver his people.

The Gospels present Jesus as that Messiah, with Mark opening his Gospel by boldly declaring: 'The beginning of the gospel about Jesus Christ, the Son of God' (Mark 1:1). However, Jesus himself was reluctant to use this title because of popular expectations about what Messiah would be and do. People were expecting a military leader who would free them from Roman oppression through miracles and might, restore and cleanse Israel, thereby preparing the way for God to establish his kingdom. But Jesus' mission was quite different; he had come to establish God's kingdom, not through a sword but through a cross. So he often commanded secrecy lest people misunderstand, though this was often ignored (e.g. Mark 1:43–45).

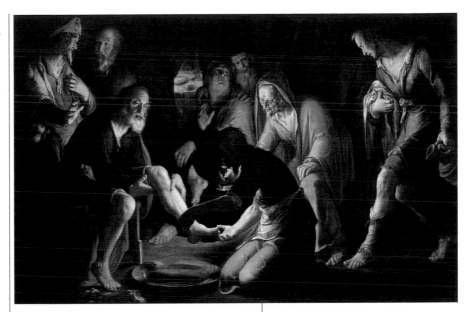

Christ Washing the Disciples' Feet, Peter Wtewael, 1623.

Servant

Probably quoting from an early Christian hymn, Paul told the Philippian church to imitate 'Christ Jesus: who, being in very nature God, did not consider equality with God something to be grasped, but made himself nothing, taking the very nature of a servant' (Philippians 2:6–7). Paul was marvelling at the mystery: the one who was with God from the beginning became not just a real human being but the lowest form of human being in those days: a servant. And it was servanthood that Jesus constantly modelled throughout his life, like when he washed his disciples' feet (John 13:1–17) or challenged their self-importance, saying, 'Whoever wants to become great among you must be your servant, and whoever wants to be first must be your slave – just as the Son of Man did not come to be served, but to serve, and to give his life as a ransom for many' (Matthew 20:26–28).

It was this ultimate aspect of servanthood – laying down one's life for another (John 15:13) – that enabled Jesus to fulfil the role of 'the Suffering Servant', prophesied by Isaiah 700 years earlier as the one who would bear Israel's sins (Isaiah 52:12 – 53:12). The Gospel writers and Jesus himself often referred to these 'Servant songs' to reinforce his claims (Matthew 8:17; Mark 9:12).

The grotto of Pan (the half-man, half-goat Greek god) at Caesarea Philippi. It was at this centre of pagan worship that Jesus asked his disciples who they thought he was. Peter replied, 'You are the Christ, the Son of the living God' (Matthew 16:16). Jesus blessed him and said that on such an insight he could build his church. That Peter didn't understand how Jesus would do this is reflected in his trying to correct Jesus when he spoke of his suffering and death; but Jesus told him, 'Get behind me, Satan! You are a stumbling-block to me; you do not have in mind the things of God, but the things of men' (Matthew 16:23).

KEY SAYING

'I am among you as one who serves.'

LUKE 22:27

His Titles: The Divine Aspect
LORD AND GOD

As we saw on the previous page, Jesus had many titles that stressed his real humanity and anointed leadership, but there were other titles that marked him out as far more than a mere man. Indeed they seem to reflect a staggering self-awareness of being nothing less than God himself; and as others began to come to the same conclusion, he never once corrected them.

Son of God

More than any other, this title (often abbreviated to simply 'the Son') highlights Jesus' *relationship* with God. Taking an already-existing title, he infused it with new meaning. In the Old Testament 'son of God' had been used of angels, Israel as a nation, or Israel's king; but Jesus boldly took it and applied it to himself. By doing this, was he therefore claiming to be divine?

There is no doubt he saw his sonship as special, applying to him in a way it didn't apply to others. Hence even with his disciples he distinguished between 'my Father and your Father, my God and your God' (John 20:17). God certainly marked him out as special, declaring at his baptism, 'You are my Son, whom I love; with you I am well pleased' (Mark 1:11), repeating similar words at his transfiguration (Mark 9:7). And Jesus constantly called God 'Father', unheard of at a personal level in Judaism, yet Jesus' favourite form of address for God (used 106 times in John's Gospel alone). He constantly referred to himself as 'the Son', a claim for which his enemies demanded he die, seeing it as blasphemous (John 19:7). All this points to Jesus having a sense of unique and intimate relationship with God. He is Son of God in a sense that cannot be said of anyone else; and it is this title, therefore, that draws a line of faith like no other.

Word

Whereas Matthew, Mark and Luke begin with Jesus' human life, John takes us behind the scenes to the cosmic dimension of who Jesus was: 'In the beginning was the Word, and the Word was with God, and the Word was God... and the Word became flesh and made his dwelling among us' (1:1,14). The term 'Word' (*Logos*) was one both Jews and Gentiles could understand, though for different reasons. Jews were very familiar with God's Word: for them, not a religious book but a dynamic reality that carried out God's will (Psalm 107:20), so much so they even personified it (Proverbs 8:22–31). For Greeks it was a philosophical term, first used by Heraclitus to designate what held an ever-changing world together and gave it order. To both Jews and Greeks, then, John was saying: this Logos you believe in, it's Jesus! He is the one who created everything, carries out God's will, holds everything together and alone makes sense of life.

During Jesus' forty days in the wilderness at the start of his ministry, Satan focused on challenging him about whether he was truly the Son of God, urging him to prove it: 'If you are the Son of God,...' (Matthew 4:1–7; Luke 4:1–13). Greek has two words for 'if', one when unsure of the answer and one when you know it already, and it is this latter that is used, underlining that, even if people might be uncertain, Satan himself had no doubts about who Jesus really was.

Jesus' temptation in the desert is portrayed in this fifteenth-century fresco.

'As the print of the seal on the wax is the express image of the seal itself, so Christ is the express image – the perfect representation of God.'
St Ambrose

Thomas said to him, 'My Lord and my God!'
JOHN 20:28

● SEE ALSO
HIS RELATIONSHIP TO GOD PP. 80–81
HIS ORIGINS PP. 24–25
HIS TITLES (HUMAN ASPECT) PP. 82–83

OTHER TITLES

Other titles of Jesus in the New Testament include:

■ Holy One

■ Lamb of God

■ Good Shepherd

■ Lion of Judah

■ Great High Priest

■ Saviour

■ Alpha and Omega (First and Last)

Lord

When Peter preached at Pentecost, he proclaimed that 'God has made this Jesus, whom you crucified, both Lord and Christ' (Acts 2:36). But it wasn't simply at this point that Jesus acquired this title 'Lord' (*Kurios*); Jesus himself had used it, like when claiming to be 'Lord of the Sabbath' (Mark 2:28), when debating with Pharisees (Matthew 22:41–46) and linking being called Lord with his right to judge (Matthew 7:21). However, it was after the resurrection that the title took on its full significance, as the disciples finally realized who Jesus was, expressed in Thomas's statement: 'My Lord and my God!' (John 20:28). Paul's use of an Aramaic creed (Aramaic was the language of Palestine) – *Maranatha!* ('Come, Lord!') – also shows that this belief that Jesus was Lord went back to the earliest days. And since *Kurios* was also used in the Greek translation of the Hebrew Bible for the name of God himself, it shows they fully understood the magnitude of what they were claiming about Jesus.

Thomas finally acknowledges Jesus as 'my Lord and my God' (John 20:28), depicted in Mattia Preti's *The Doubting or Incredulity of Saint Thomas*.

This title, in fact, became the central confession of Christianity, Paul saying that 'if you confess with your mouth, Jesus is Lord, and believe in your heart that God raised him from the dead, you will be saved' (Romans 10:9). That sounded easy enough, but when Roman emperors started claiming they were God, it became a battle ground. The final straw came when the emperor demanded everyone take an oath of allegiance, declaring 'Caesar is Lord'. Christians couldn't do it, because for them there was only one Lord, Jesus. Their refusal to comply led to thousands being tortured and killed. Such was their commitment to the belief that Jesus was indeed God, the eternal Lord.

KEY SAYING

'You will see the Son of Man sitting at the right hand of the Mighty One and coming on the clouds of heaven.'

MARK 14:62

His Transfiguration
GLORY BREAKING THROUGH

The Western world generally doesn't cope well with the mysterious, preferring to look for scientific explanations for everything but then shrugging its shoulders when science can't provide them. Jesus' life was full of the mysterious, some of it explainable, some not. But one event was certainly more mysterious and unexplainable than any other: his transfiguration, when the glory he had left in heaven could no longer be contained and, for a moment, burst through into our world.

What Happened?

A week after Peter realized that Jesus was the Messiah (Matthew 16:13–28), Jesus took Peter, James and John up a mountain where they discovered something even more amazing about him. When they were alone, Jesus 'was transfigured' (Matthew 17:2; Mark 9:2). The Greek is the word from which our word 'metamorphosis' comes; so whatever exactly happened, it was a mysterious and amazing 'transformation' as heaven's glory broke through and found its home on the one to whom it belonged. Matthew tells us Jesus' face 'shone like the sun' (Matthew 17:2) and Mark, recording Peter's eyewitness memories, wrote that 'his clothes became dazzling white, whiter than anyone in the world could bleach them' (Mark 9:2).

And then two key Old Testament characters, Moses and Elijah, suddenly appeared, discussing 'his departure, which he was about to bring to fulfilment at Jerusalem' (Luke 9:31); that is, his impending death and its significance, for the word 'departure' actually means 'exodus'. They knew that what Jesus was about to do would bring about a deliverance on the scale of that brought about by Moses when he freed God's people from slavery in Egypt.

But it wasn't over yet. Suddenly 'a bright cloud enveloped them, and a voice from the cloud said, "This is my Son, whom I love; with him I am well pleased. Listen to him!"' (Matthew 17:5) – a confirmation to Jesus of his Father's love and purpose as the journey to the cross was about to begin, and a revelation to them of who this man really was.

The Transfiguration, c. 1500–21, by Giovanni Girolamo Savoldo.

Old Testament Echoes

The transfiguration was full of echoes of the Old Testament, which Jesus said he came to fulfil (Matthew 5:17):

■ Moses and Elijah
Both had heard God on a mountain (Exodus 24:15–18; 1 Kings 19:8–18); now both bore witness to what God had to say to Jesus on another mountain, together representing the Old Covenant which pointed to him. Both had passed from this life mysteriously: Moses was buried by God unseen (Deuteronomy 34:5–6) and Elijah taken to heaven by a whirlwind (2 Kings 2:11–21); both now returned just as mysteriously to honour the one whose revelation theirs had prepared for.

■ The mountain
For Jews mountains and deserts were significant in their history, especially Mount Sinai, where God gave the Law to Moses during their wilderness journey (Exodus 19:1). As Moses encountered the glory of God on Mount Sinai, so now Jesus encountered that same glory on this mountain, as a new and better 'Moses'.

■ The cloud
Clouds often symbolized the glorious presence of God in the Old Testament. It was a cloud that led Israel through the wilderness (Exodus 13:21–22); a cloud that symbolized God's presence at Sinai (Exodus 19:16–19); a cloud that covered the tabernacle when it was consecrated (Exodus 40:34–35); a cloud on which Daniel saw the Son of man arriving (Daniel 7:13). Now here was that same cloud, speaking of God's glory in Jesus.

● SEE ALSO
HIS ORIGINS PP. 24–25
HIS RELATIONSHIP TO GOD PP. 80–81
SON OF GOD P. 84

He received honour and glory from God the Father when the voice came to him from the Majestic Glory, saying, 'This is my Son, whom I love; with him I am well pleased.'

2 PETER 1:17

WHERE DID IT HAPPEN?

This representation of the transfiguration is in the Church of the Transfiguration on Mount Tabor, the site of this event according to the Early Church Fathers. However, they were almost certainly wrong, their identification being based on a misreading of the Greek text. Moreover, Jesus had been near Caesarea Philippi just prior to the transfiguration, a considerable distance from Tabor; so a far more likely location was nearby Mount Hermon, just 12 miles (20 km) to the north-east.

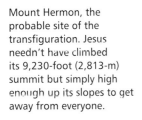

Mount Hermon, the probable site of the transfiguration. Jesus needn't have climbed its 9,230-foot (2,813-m) summit but simply high enough up its slopes to get away from everyone.

The Disciples' Reaction

Not surprisingly, the transfiguration left the disciples terrified and needing Jesus' reassurance (Matthew 17:6–7). It wasn't just their encounter with the supernatural world, but what they feared might be about to happen. As Jews they had been taught that the righteous dead would all be resurrected simultaneously; but if Moses and Elijah were there, then this probably meant the End was right now. If so, were they ready? Moreover they were confused, for didn't the Scriptures say Elijah would appear before Messiah's coming (Malachi 4:5), a question they put to Jesus later (Matthew 17:10)? But Jesus replied that the Elijah figure had in fact already appeared, in the form of John the Baptist (Matthew 17:11–13).

The impact of this event never left Peter. Even looking back on it thirty years later, his sense of amazement, yet conviction it had really happened, still comes out: *'We did not follow cleverly invented stories when we told you about the power and coming of our Lord Jesus Christ, but we were eye-witnesses of his majesty. For he received honour and glory from God the Father when the voice came to him from the Majestic Glory, saying, "This is my Son, whom I love; with him I am well pleased." We ourselves heard this voice that came from heaven when we were with him on the sacred mountain'* (2 Peter 1:16–18).

KEY SAYING

'Some who are standing here will not taste death before they see the kingdom of God come with power.'

MARK 9:1

87

His Dependence

LOOKING TO GOD

Even before Jesus' birth there had been a flurry of the Spirit's activity as there hadn't been for centuries (Luke 1:11–17, 26–38, 41, 67). And then, having been conceived by the Spirit, Jesus was totally dependent on him thereafter. It was the Spirit who filled him at his baptism, led him into the wilderness, brought him back to Nazareth, commissioned him for ministry, brought his Father's resources and, ultimately, led him to the cross. Having laid aside his glory in the incarnation, Jesus knew that without God's Spirit, he could do nothing.

Filled with the Spirit

The Gospels tell us that Jesus was baptized by John (Matthew 3:13–17; Mark 1:9–11; Luke 3:21–22; John 1:29–34) the Gospels tell us that heaven was opened (Mark's Greek text says it was 'split apart'), and God's Spirit came and rested on Jesus 'like a dove'. Interestingly they didn't say it was a dove that came, but rather that the Spirit came like a dove, the nearest eyewitnesses at the time could get to describing the phenomenon they saw that day (rather like the nearest they could get to describing the Spirit's coming at Pentecost was 'like the blowing of a violent wind', Acts 2:2). This was the moment when Jesus was filled with God's Spirit, and it was only from this point onwards that his ministry, and his miracles, began. Until now he had been able to do nothing, for he simply didn't have the resources; but now, 'full of the Holy Spirit' (Luke 4:1), he was ready to demonstrate his complete dependence on his Father and his word through the trial of the temptations (Luke 4:2–13) before returning to Nazareth 'in the power of the Spirit' (Luke 4:14), ready to begin his work.

Gifts of the Spirit

Christians are accustomed to hearing of the gifts of the Spirit in Paul's writings (Romans 12:4–8; 1 Corinthians 12:7–11, 27–31), but the Gospels also show Jesus using many of those gifts himself: not just healing and deliverance but also things like words of knowledge (Matthew 9:4; John 4:16–18), words of wisdom (Matthew 22:15–22; John 8:6–7) and prophecy (Luke 18:31; John 13:38), all showing that he too had to depend on the Spirit and his gifts.

THE ANOINTING OF THE SPIRIT

Olive oil, produced from the plentiful olives that grew in Palestine, was used in Old Testament times for anointing prophets, priests and kings to symbolize the outpouring of God's Spirit that could alone enable them to do what God had called them to. Jesus referred to this practice when he went to the synagogue in Nazareth and read from Isaiah's prophecy of how Messiah would be utterly dependent on God and his Spirit: 'The Spirit of the Lord is on me, because he has anointed me to preach good news to the poor. He has sent me to proclaim freedom for the prisoners and recovery of sight for the blind, to release the oppressed, to proclaim the year of the Lord's favour' (Luke 4:18–19). Jesus was declaring that his ministry would meet every human need, just as Isaiah had prophesied, but also that the only way he could do it would be by utter dependence on God's Spirit.

> The Spirit of the LORD will rest on him – the Spirit of wisdom and of understanding, the Spirit of counsel and of power, the Spirit of knowledge and of the fear of the LORD.
>
> ISAIAH **11:2**

● SEE ALSO
BAPTISM P. 113
HIS ORIGINS PP. 24–25
HIS RELATIONSHIP TO GOD PP. 80–81

Why Did Jesus Need the Spirit?

An obvious question is that if Jesus really were God incarnate, why did he need anything or anyone else? Why could he do nothing until filled with the Holy Spirit? The answer is to do with the reality of the incarnation. Paul summed it up like this: 'Christ Jesus who, being in very nature God, did not consider equality with God something to be grasped, but made himself nothing, taking the very nature of a servant, being made in human likeness' (Philippians 2:6–7). That phrase 'made himself nothing' literally means 'emptied himself'. By some mystery we cannot even begin to understand, Jesus 'emptied himself' of his divine power and glory to become a real human being; the same person he had always been, but in an utterly different mode of existence. So now as a perfect human being, 'a new Adam' as Paul puts it (Romans 5; 1 Corinthians 15), Jesus had no inner hidden resources of his own; all he could do was depend on God, just as the first Adam was meant to do but didn't. Jesus did his miracles then, not in his own power, but by complete dependence on the Spirit and obedience to his Father.

THE ULTIMATE DEPENDENCE

'And if the Spirit of him who raised Jesus from the dead is living in you, he who raised Christ from the dead will also give life to your mortal bodies through his Spirit, who lives in you' (Romans 8:11).

Jesus' ultimate dependence was when he entrusted himself to God in death, having no intrinsic power of his own to conquer death but trusting God's Spirit to raise him after he died. Christians often speak of Jesus 'rising from the dead', but actually the New Testament far more commonly speaks of him 'being raised' from the dead, underlining it was not him who did it but his Father.

Dependence and Discipleship

Jesus was not only dependent on God and his Spirit himself; he wanted his disciples to depend on them too, just as he had done. That's why he promised he would send the Holy Spirit to them (John 14:15–27; 16:5–16), a promise he repeated before his ascension (Acts 1:4–8) and kept on the day of Pentecost (Acts 2:1–4).

In this fresco in the Byzantine St Saviour in Chora Church, Istanbul, Jesus has been resurrected and has broken down the gates of hell. He is pulling Adam and Eve from their tombs.

KEY SAYING

'I tell you the truth, the Son can do nothing by himself; he can do only what he sees his Father doing.'

JOHN 5:19

His Battle
OVERCOMING EVIL

From the very beginning of Jesus' earthly life, Satan did his best to destroy him. The first attempt was just after his birth, when Herod ordered the slaughter of male babies in Bethlehem (Matthew 2:16–18). Many other attempts followed, such as Satan's tempting Jesus to jump from the top of the Temple (Luke 4:9) and the crowd in Nazareth trying to throw him from the cliff (Luke 4:29). But while Satan constantly opposed Jesus, fearful of what he had come to do and determined to resist him, Jesus said that he was already defeated.

Satan's Origins

Satan first appears in the Bible in the Garden of Eden as a serpent (Genesis 3). But where did he come from, if God's creation was perfect? The Bible seems to say that he was a high-ranking angel who rebelled against God and was cast out of heaven (Isaiah 14:12–15; Ezekiel 28:12–19), along with one-third of the angels, who also rebelled (Revelation 12:4). (That means there are far more angels than demons if only a third fell!) Ever since, Satan has sought to oppose God, his purposes and his people; but his ultimate and complete overthrow is assured (Matthew 25:41; Revelation 20:7–10).

THE TEMPTATIONS

One of Jesus' first battles with Satan was during his forty-day fast in the wilderness where Jesus overcame him by quoting God's word (Luke 4:1–13). Satan then 'left him until an opportune time'.

The third temptation, portrayed here by William Blake, required Jesus to throw himself off a pinnacle.

The Stronger Man

No matter how uneasily it might sit with Western worldviews, freeing people from Satan's grip was an integral aspect of Jesus' work. Peter, looking back in one of his sermons, remembered how Jesus 'went around doing good and healing all who were under the power of the devil' (Acts 10:38). For him, freeing people from Satan's grip was an indispensable part of Jesus' doing good.

A key aspect of his battle against Satan was through exorcisms, freeing people from demonic powers that gripped them. Jesus summed up their significance like this: 'How can anyone enter a strong man's house and carry off his possessions unless he first ties up the strong man? Then he can rob his house' (Matthew 12:29). In other words, through these exorcisms he was binding Satan in preparation for plundering his property, reclaiming what he had stolen (John 10:10) as the first stage in his ultimate defeat. While that wouldn't happen until the cross, the outcome was so assured that, even before that event, Jesus could say, 'Now is the time for judgment on this world; now the prince of this world will be driven out' (John 12:31).

He went around doing good and healing all who were under the power of the devil, because God was with him.

ACTS **10:38**

Demons

For Jesus, 'evil' was not something impersonal but personal, rooted in Satan and expressed through demons who serve him. Demons' presence in people was often characterized by screaming, convulsions, unpredictable behaviour, and unusual strength; but while they were strong, Jesus was stronger (Luke 11:21–22), as demonstrated in his exorcisms, an expression of his mission to free people from whatever bound them (Luke 4:18–19).

While numerous exorcisms are mentioned in the Gospels, only four are described at length:

■ **The man in the Capernaum synagogue** (Mark 1:21–28), whose demon recognized Jesus was God. Jesus rebuked the demon, telling it to leave the man, which happened immediately and dramatically.

■ **The Gerasene man with many demons** (Mark 5:1–20), who was violent and lived among tombs. Jesus freed him by casting the demons into nearby pigs, which leapt off the cliff.

■ **The Syro-Phoenician woman's daughter** (Mark 7:24–30), who was freed from a demon at a distance.

■ **The boy with a deaf and dumb spirit** (Mark 9:14–29). Jesus commanded the spirit to leave, which it did, instantly and dramatically.

While both Jewish and Gentile exorcists were common in ancient times (e.g. Mark 9:38–40), Jesus differed from them significantly. First, he drove out demons by his own authority, not in the name of some other deity; second, he didn't use set methods (whether apparatus or phraseology) but delivered people in a variety of ways; third, he didn't pray but simply commanded the demons to leave.

Jesus not only cast out demons himself but sent his disciples to do the same (Mark 3:14–15).

In League with the Devil?

Some of Jesus' opponents accused him of doing miracles by being in league with Satan (Matthew 12:24). Jesus showed the folly of this argument: why would Satan want to cast out himself? It would only weaken his kingdom (Matthew 12:25–26). On the contrary, Jesus' victory over demons showed that God's kingdom was truly here (12:28), and he warned them of the danger of ascribing to the devil what God was doing (12:31–32).

NAMES OF SATAN

Satan has various names in the Bible:

■ **Satan** (Matthew 4:10), meaning 'Accuser' or 'Adversary'

■ **The devil** (Matthew 4:1), Greek translation of Satan

■ **Lucifer** (Isaiah 14:12, KJV), meaning 'Morning Star', 'Shining One'

■ **Beelzebub** (Mark 3:22), meaning 'Lord of the flies' (parodying Baal-Zebub, 'Exalted Lord', Baal being a Canaanite god)

■ **Evil one** (Matthew 13:19), reflecting his work

Ruins of the fifth-century church and monastery at Kursi (Gerasa), on the eastern shore of the Sea of Galilee, built to commemorate Jesus freeing the man with many demons (Mark 5:1–20). Unusually, Jesus demanded

the demon's name, the man (or demon) replying, 'My name is Legion, for we are many.' Whether he was speaking literally (a Roman legion had about 6,000 soldiers) or metaphorically (meaning a complexity of demons) is of little importance; the point of the story is that Jesus completely freed him, casting the demons into nearby pigs (for Jews, unclean animals, thereby highlighting the uncleanness of the demons), perhaps so the man could really know he was free at last. Everyone certainly recognized the miraculous change in him (Mark 5:15–17).

KEY SAYING

'*I saw Satan fall like lightning from heaven.*'

LUKE 10:18

His Opponents
RESISTING JESUS

Strange as it may seem, the man who came to establish God's kingdom on earth was opposed, not by representatives of earthly kingdoms who might have had due cause to fear him, but by religious leaders who felt they were the guardians of that very kingdom Jesus came to bring. What troubled them was Jesus' claim that this kingdom was coming in a way so different from what they expected, and above all that it was coming through *him*. And so they got rid of him.

Religious Opponents

Jesus' main opponents were the religious elite of his day:

■ Pharisees

Deeply aware of their history, which told them that Israel's disobedience had led to exile, the Pharisees saw that scrupulous obedience to God's Law was the duty of every Jew, and they sought to lead the way. They not only kept the 613 commandments the rabbis had identified in it, but also a host of additional oral traditions. It was the latter that brought them into constant conflict with Jesus, especially over what they saw as crucial identity markers like ritual washings, fasting, tithing, Sabbath-keeping and avoiding anything, or anyone, defiling. But Jesus rejected their rituals and traditions as undermining the very heart of what God had intended (Matthew 5:21–48) and berated their hypocrisy (Matthew 23:1–39).

■ Sadducees

The Sadducees controlled the high priesthood and the Temple, and were afraid of Jesus lest he upset the status quo and destroy the delicate political balance which would lead to a loss of influence. But they also had theological disagreements with him, like the issue of the resurrection of the dead (Mark 12:18–27) and his attitude to the Temple (Matthew 26:59–61). While they had little in common with the Pharisees, politically or theologically, they sometimes joined them in opposing Jesus. It was their man Caiaphas, the high priest, who was ultimately responsible for ensuring the execution of Jesus (John 18:14).

■ Scribes

Scribes had taken on new significance during the Jewish exile in Babylon, when priests were no longer required because the Temple lay hundreds of miles away in ruins, and so the Law, the only thing that Jews now had left, became even more important. The scribes began to interpret that Law for the new situation Jews found themselves in, and by New Testament times their interpretations were seen as important as the Law itself. Jesus angered them by rejecting those interpretations and suggesting they had 'let go of the commands of God and are holding on to the traditions of men' (Mark 7:8), which provoked their opposition; but he felt they had become over-concerned with detail to the exclusion of the big issues in life (Matthew 15:1–20).

John's Gospel often groups together all these religious leaders, describing them simply as 'the Jews'.

The Pharisees and Herodians take counsel against Jesus, as portrayed in this painting by James Tissot.

The Pharisees and the teachers of the law began to oppose him fiercely.

LUKE 11:53

SEE ALSO
HIS ATTITUDE TO RELIGION PP. 74–75
PHARISEES P. 18
SADDUCEES P. 18

Political Opponents

Surprisingly, Jesus had very few political opponents. This may have been because he kept a low profile in Galilee for most of the time and because he made it clear he hadn't come to oppose Rome like many of his fellow Jews were wanting. But politics wasn't his concern; God's kingdom was. Hence he had no problem telling people to pay their Roman taxes (Mark 12:13–17) or to carry Roman soldiers' packs (Matthew 5:41); it was simply irrelevant to his purpose.

■ King Herod

Herod had inevitably heard about Jesus and had responded with a mixture of curiosity (Luke 9:7–9), opposition (Luke 13:3) and a desire to see a miracle (Luke 23:8); but he only ever met Jesus on the eve of his death (Luke 23:7–12), and Jesus refused to answer a single one of his questions.

■ The Herodians

These supporters of Herod were hoping for his rule to be restored in Judea (currently governed by Pilate), so were troubled by anyone who might cause Rome to tighten its direct control. They often tried to catch Jesus out, like over the issue of paying taxes to Caesar (Matthew 22:15–22). From very early in Jesus' ministry the Herodians and Pharisees (strange bedfellows indeed) often plotted together against him (Mark 3:6), though for very different reasons.

■ The Romans

Rome never saw Jesus as a threat. For them he was just another rabbi with yet another variant of those superstitious Jewish ideas. In fact Romans come out rather well in the Gospels: one centurion was commended by Jesus for his faith (Luke 7:1–10), and another esteemed him at the cross (Matthew 27:54; Luke 23:47). Even though it was Pilate who ultimately sanctioned Jesus' death, the Gospels show it was the religious leaders who were primarily responsible for it, as Peter boldly declared in his Pentecost sermon (Acts 2:13–15).

Methods of Opposition

■ Physical violence (Luke 4:28–30)

■ Trick questions (Matthew 22:15–22)

■ Trying to corner him (John 8:1–11)

■ Theological debate (Luke 20:27–39)

■ Turning his words against him (Mark 14:57–59)

■ Putting him under oath (Matthew 26:62–63)

While Jesus responded, he never reacted, always seeking to live by his own teaching that we should love our enemies (Matthew 5:44–48).

Surprising Opponents

Sometimes Jesus' opponents came from unexpected quarters. This included his own family, as we see with his brothers who didn't believe in him (John 7:1–5) and who came to Capernaum to take him home (Mark 3:31–32). It also included Peter who, having been commended for his insight, suddenly found himself being called Satan for attempting to deflect Jesus from his path (Matthew 16:22–23).

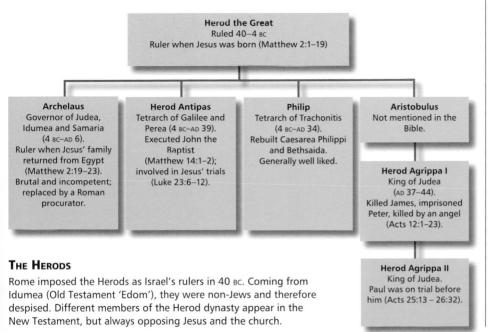

Herod the Great
Ruled 40–4 BC
Ruler when Jesus was born (Matthew 2:1–19)

Archelaus
Governor of Judea, Idumea and Samaria (4 BC–AD 6).
Ruler when Jesus' family returned from Egypt (Matthew 2:19–23). Brutal and incompetent; replaced by a Roman procurator.

Herod Antipas
Tetrarch of Galilee and Perea (4 BC–AD 39).
Executed John the Baptist (Matthew 14:1–2); involved in Jesus' trials (Luke 23:6–12).

Philip
Tetrarch of Trachonitis (4 BC–AD 34).
Rebuilt Caesarea Philippi and Bethsaida. Generally well liked.

Aristobulus
Not mentioned in the Bible.

Herod Agrippa I
King of Judea (AD 37–44).
Killed James, imprisoned Peter, killed by an angel (Acts 12:1–23).

Herod Agrippa II
King of Judea.
Paul was on trial before him (Acts 25:13 – 26:32).

THE HERODS

Rome imposed the Herods as Israel's rulers in 40 BC. Coming from Idumea (Old Testament 'Edom'), they were non-Jews and therefore despised. Different members of the Herod dynasty appear in the New Testament, but always opposing Jesus and the church.

> **KEY SAYING**
>
> *'Love your enemies and pray for those who persecute you.'*
>
> MATTHEW 5:44

His Final Week
THE GOAL APPROACHES

Three years of showing people what God was really like, three years of kindness and miracles and amazing teaching, suddenly came to a climax in one final action-packed week. While he had blessed many, Jesus had also crossed the religious leaders; so they conspired to dispose of him once and for all. And yet, though it looked as if they had the upper hand, everything about that final week spoke of Jesus being mysteriously in control.

MARY ANOINTING JESUS' FEET

Honouring important guests by anointing their heads wasn't unusual; but Jesus saw Mary's anointing of him as particularly significant. While Judas complained the perfume could have been sold and the money given to the poor, Jesus saw the gesture as prophetic: 'She poured perfume on my body beforehand to prepare for my burial' (Mark 14:8). He knew that when the time for burial came there would be no opportunity for such niceties.

EVENTS OF HOLY WEEK

1. Friday: Arrival in Bethany

Jesus arrived in Bethany, a tiny hamlet of around twenty homes, staying with his friends Lazarus, Mary and Martha (John 12:1). Mary anointed his feet with expensive perfume, which Jesus saw as preparation for his burial (John 12:2–8).

2. Saturday: Rest Day

While no details are given in the Gospels, Jesus probably spent his final Sabbath relaxing with his friends in Bethany.

3. Sunday: Triumphal Entry

Borrowing a donkey from nearby Bethphage (Matthew 21:1), Jesus rode into Jerusalem, fulfilling Zechariah's prophecy (Zechariah 9:9). Crowds gathered, waving palm branches, welcoming him as their king and shouting 'Hosanna!' (Matthew 21:1–11; Mark 11:1–11; Luke 19:28–44; John 12:12–16). Jesus wept over Jerusalem's tragic destiny (Luke 19:41–44).

4. Monday: Cleansing the Temple

Jesus returned to Jerusalem from Bethany, cursing a fruitless fig tree on the way (Mark 11:12–14). Arriving at the Temple, he was outraged to find its outer courtyard full of traders and money-changers. He threw them out and overturned their tables (Matthew 21:12–17; Mark 11:12–19; Luke 19:45–46).

5. Tuesday: Teaching

Returning to the Temple, Jesus taught all who would listen, though the religious leaders were still challenging him (Matthew 21:23 – 23:39; Mark 11:27 – 12:44; Luke 20:1 – 21:4). Later he left for the Mount of Olives where he spoke about Jerusalem's destruction and his return at the end of the age (Matthew 24:1 – 25:46; Mark 13:1–37; Luke 21:5–38).

6. Wednesday: Teaching

The Gospels don't specify what happened today, though Jesus probably continued teaching.

THE TRIUMPHAL ENTRY

For pilgrims seeing Jerusalem as they came over the Mount of Olives, the atmosphere was always electric; but it was even more so that day as Jesus rode into the city. Underlining how his messianic claims were different from those expected, he rode not a horse (an animal of war) but a donkey (an animal of peace). And yet, there was more; for Zechariah had prophesied that Israel's king would enter Jerusalem riding a donkey (Zechariah 9:9). The crowds formed a guard of honour, waving palm branches (victory symbols), laying their cloaks on the road, and welcoming him as the one who 'comes in the name of the Lord' and crying 'Hosanna' ('Save!'). They were consciously acknowledging him as king, though their cries would change by Friday when he didn't fulfil their expectations.

● **SEE ALSO**
GETHSEMANE P. 98
THE LAST SUPPER P. 96
THE TEMPLE P. 17

The chief priests and Pharisees had given orders that if anyone found out where Jesus was, he should report it so that they might arrest him.

JOHN 11:57

7. Thursday: Last Supper and Gethsemane

After washing his disciples' feet, Jesus celebrated Passover with them one day early, for he knew he wouldn't be alive the next day. Judas went off to betray him while the rest of them left for Gethsemane where Jesus predicted Peter's denial and prayed, waiting to be arrested (Matthew 26:31–56; Mark 14:27–52; Luke 22:31–53; John 18:1–14).

CURSING THE FIG TREE

Hungry as he returned to Jerusalem, Jesus saw a fig tree in full leaf so went to pick figs (Mark 11:12–14). When he saw it had no fruit 'because it was not the season for figs', he cursed it. Although this seems unreasonable (why expect fruit out of season?), it was unusual for a fig tree to even have all its leaves at that time of year; that shouldn't have happened for another two months when its leaves would have shown its fruit was ready. This picture of false hope was just like Israel, and his cursing the tree was a prophetic sign of the coming judgment on a spiritually fruitless nation.

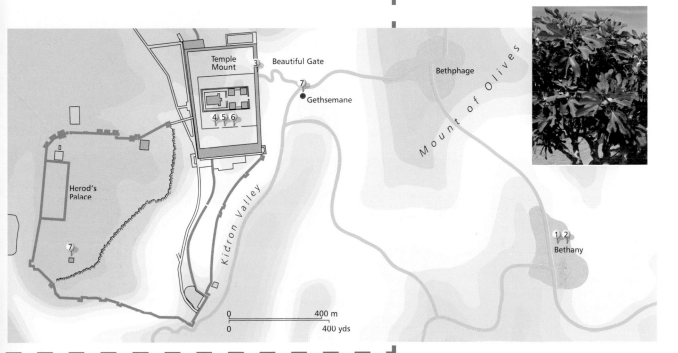

CLEANSING THE TEMPLE

Jesus had already cleansed the Temple early in his ministry (John 2:12–22), but vested interests led to malpractice creeping in again and the Court of the Gentiles had become a mere marketplace. Jesus drove out the merchants and animals and upturned the money-changers' tables (Matthew 21:12–17; Mark 11:15–19; Luke 19:45–46), saying they had turned a house of prayer into a den of robbers. Through this action Jesus was:

■ Showing concern for Gentiles since this was the only part of the Temple where they could pray

■ Opposing financial corruption, since the Temple depended on extortionate prices and exchange rates

■ Declaring that the Temple's days were numbered and judgment was coming

Increasing Plots

• •

Increasingly angry, the religious leaders gathered in the high priest's house and plotted to arrest Jesus. '"But not during the Feast," they said, "or there may be a riot among the people"' (Matthew 26:4–5). Jesus, aware of their intentions, told the parable of the tenants to their delegation (Matthew 21:33–46). The parable climaxed in the tenants killing the master's son, an obvious reference to them and him. So they 'looked for a way to arrest him immediately, because they knew he had spoken this parable against them. But they were afraid of the people' (Luke 20:19).

KEY SAYING

'The stone the builders rejected has become the capstone.'

MARK 12:10

His Final Meal
A NEW PASSOVER

Together with Pentecost and Tabernacles, Passover was one of the three main Jewish festivals. Hundreds of thousands of pilgrims, not just from Palestine but the wider Jewish dispersion, flocked to Jerusalem for it, and many of them, like Jesus and his disciples, had to sleep in nearby villages or bivouac on the Mount of Olives. But with such a crowd, where would they even find a place to celebrate Passover? Jesus had it all in hand, however; for not only was a room prepared, the whole scenario was.

JESUS THE SERVANT

Before the meal, Jesus washed his disciples' feet (John 13:1–17). No servant was there to perform this common courtesy for travellers, and no one else volunteered to do it, so Jesus took off his outer garment, wrapped a towel round his waist and did it himself. Passover was eaten reclining, the feet away from the table; so Jesus went around the outside of the circle washing each disciple's feet. In doing this Jesus was not only demonstrating humility, but also prefiguring his death as Isaiah's prophesied Suffering Servant (Isaiah 53).

Jesus' Last Supper with his disciples is portrayed in this 1803 painting after Leonardo da Vinci.

The Last Supper

It was Thursday 14 Nisan, and the priests had been slaughtering Passover lambs all afternoon. Normally Passover would be celebrated the next day, but since for Jews each day ended at sunset, and since Jesus knew he wouldn't be around the next day to celebrate it, he shared it with his disciples on the evening of the 14th instead. With the authorities now looking to arrest him, a secure

location for it was important, so he sent his disciples ahead to an upper room in Jerusalem that he had previously organized where they could prepare the Passover meal (Matthew 26:17–19; Mark 14:12–16; Luke 22:7–13).

By Jesus' time, Passover had become central to Jewish self-understanding. Not only did it look back, reliving the story of the exodus, it also looked forward to God's rescuing his people once again, this time not from Egypt but from their Roman masters. But Jesus was about to give it a whole new meaning. At first, everything seemed to be following the old traditions, when suddenly Jesus changed the wording over the bread and wine ('the bread of affliction' and 'the

cup of redemption'), giving the meal a new twist by placing his body and his blood at the centre of Israel's story and, by implication, claiming he was about to bring the new exodus for which Israel had been longing. But not only was there to be a new exodus, there was also to be a new covenant, established by him between God and people that would bring about the forgiveness of sins (Matthew 26:28).

● SEE ALSO
HIS TEACHING: HOLY SPIRIT PP. 50–51
JESUS THE SERVANT P. 83
PASSOVER PP. 96–97

THE UPPER ROOM

Although this building visited by tourists as the location of the Upper Room actually dates from the twelfth century, there is evidence of early Christian presence on this site, so it may well be in the general area of the actual Upper Room. It was in the Upper Room that Jesus predicted Peter would deny him three times (Matthew 26:31–35; Mark 14:27–31; Luke 22:31–34).

REMEMBERING TODAY

Jesus' command that his disciples should 'do this in remembrance of me' (Luke 22:19) quickly led to the sharing of bread and wine becoming a key part of Christian worship, though initially this was in the context of a meal (Acts 2:46). Today Christians around the world still share bread and wine to remember his death, but call it by different names (the Lord's Supper, Holy Communion, Mass) and celebrate it in very different styles, from the very informal to the heavily ritualistic, as seen in these photos.

Judas' Betrayal

During the meal Judas slipped out, going to the high priest's house which was nearby to arrange Jesus' betrayal. He had been looking for the right moment for several days (Matthew 26:14–16; Mark 10:2; Luke 22:1–6), ever since the anointing in Bethany which had so angered him, and it was perhaps Jesus' own talk about his death that gave him confidence to now act. Jesus knew his intentions, however (Matthew 26:20–25; Mark 14:17–21; Luke 22:22–23; John 13:18–30), and their reclining positions enabled John to ascertain quietly from him the identity of the betrayer (John 13:23–26).

Why such a close disciple should betray Jesus is hard to understand. Yes, Satan was involved (Luke 22:3; John 13:27); but Judas had also failed to deal with a basic character weakness. While some suggest he was trying to force Jesus' hand into acting against the Romans, the only psychological insight the Gospels offer is that, provoked by what he perceived as the waste of money at Jesus' anointing, he simply did it for the money (Matthew 26:8–9, 14–16). Not that he gained much, as thirty pieces of silver was only the value of a slave, or about four months' wages. Later, troubled by his conscience, he tried to return the money, but when the religious leaders washed their hands of it, he committed suicide (Matthew 27:1–5).

Jesus' Final Teaching

Knowing this would be his last opportunity, Jesus underlined some key issues to his disciples, described at some length in John's Gospel (chapters 13–17). These included: the importance of loving and serving one another (13:1–17; 15:17), a reminder that everything is possible through faith (14:5–14), the coming of the Holy Spirit (14:15–30; 16:5–16), the importance of bearing fruit (15:1–16), being ready to face opposition (15:18 – 16:4) and preparation for their coming sadness (16:17–33). Jesus then prayed for himself, them and all future disciples (chapter 17) before leaving for Gethsemane where he would be arrested.

KEY SAYING

'This is my body given for you; do this in remembrance of me... This cup is the new covenant in my blood, which is poured out for you.'

LUKE 22:19–20

His Final Evening
THE GARDEN AND THE CUP

Most people, knowing death was coming, would run; but Jesus didn't, convinced this was why he had come to this world. He went to a favourite spot, the Garden of Gethsemane on the Mount of Olives, just across the valley from Jerusalem, where he prayed, 'My Father, if it is possible, may this cup be taken from me. Yet not as I will, but as you will' (Matthew 26:39). But he already knew the answer; so he waited.

GETHSEMANE

Olive trees in Gethsemane on the Mount of Olives which was covered with olive trees in Jesus' time. Even though they can survive for hundreds of years, probably none remain from his day, since Josephus tells us that the Romans destroyed them all during the siege of Jerusalem in AD 70.

Jesus Prays

Lit by the full moon, and probably with Passover songs ringing from nearby homes, Jesus and his disciples left Jerusalem for the Garden of Gethsemane on the other side of the Kidron Valley. Leaving his disciples to rest, he asked Peter, James and John to come with him while he prayed; but weariness overtook them and they kept falling asleep (Matthew 26:36–46; Mark 14:32–42; Luke 22:39–46).

Gethsemane ('oil press') was a highly appropriate name in the light of the crushing experience that Jesus then underwent, his sweat dripping like drops of blood (Luke 22:44). What caused him such anguish was not simply knowing he was about to be crucified the next day, but also knowing that he would bear the sin of the whole world. Little wonder he asked his Father if there were any other plan. Here was a reflection of Jesus' humanity, but also his absolute trust of his Father as he submitted to his will. The issue firmly resolved, he got up to await his betrayer.

Giovanni Bellini portrays Jesus praying in the Garden of Gethsemane while Peter, James and John sleep.

Since Gethsemane means 'oil press', olives were probably processed as well as grown there. Ripe olives were first crushed into pulp by a millstone, as in this example. The crushed pulp was placed in thick baskets, stacked on top of one another with a heavy stone slab on top. A beam was placed on the stone from which heavy weights were suspended, the pressure squeezing the oil from the pulp to be collected into jars. The oil was used for cooking, fuel and as a skin lotion. Pickled olives were eaten, and olive wood was carved and polished into fine furniture.

They went to a place called Gethsemane.
Mark 14:32

SEE ALSO
HIS PRAYING PP. 72–73
JUDAS' BETRAYAL P. 97
MOUNT OF OLIVES PP. 49, 98

'Let This Cup Pass from Me'

While this prayer is often interpreted as though Jesus were saying, 'May I be spared this hard experience', his real meaning was far deeper. Jesus was referring to 'the cup of God's wrath', an image used by the prophets in which God was pictured with a goblet that was storing up his wrath – his righteous anger against sin – to be poured out on his enemies on the Last Day (e.g. Psalm 75:8; Isaiah 51:17–23; Jeremiah 25:15–28). But Jesus was saying it was *he* who was going to drink that judgment instead. Little wonder he faced such inner agony, asking his Father if there might be another way. However, the New Testament never suggests this was something the Father forced upon his Son, but rather a plan of perfect co-operation.

View of Jerusalem from Gethsemane. As Jesus sat in Gethsemane he would have had a clear view across the Kidron Valley of the crowd coming to arrest him, their flaming torches obvious in the darkness. He could easily have fled east towards Bethany; yet rather than run, he quietly awaited their arrival and his arrest.

The Arrest

Jesus didn't wait for his betrayer but rather went out to meet him (Matthew 26:46), such was his confidence that everything lay in his Father's hands. As Judas arrived, he identified Jesus to the crowd, a mixture of rabble, priests, elders and Temple guards, with a pre-arranged signal: a kiss, a hypocritical cover for his malign intent. Peter tried to defend Jesus by striking out with a sword, cutting off the ear of a servant; but Jesus, compassionate to the end, healed him and told Peter to put away his sword, saying he could call on twelve legions of angels if force was how God wanted to do things. With that, he let them lead him away, while the disciples fled. Jesus was now truly alone. (See Matthew 26:47–56; Mark 14:43–52; Luke 22:47–53; John 18:1–11.)

'A young man, wearing nothing but a linen garment, was following Jesus. When they seized him, he fled naked, leaving his garment behind' (Mark 14:51–52).
The man's anonymity suggests it was John Mark, the author of Mark's Gospel and close companion of Peter, upon whose memoirs his Gospel was based.

Roman steps leading from Jerusalem's Upper City down to the Kidron Valley. It is likely these were the very steps that Jesus took on his final journey to Gethsemane and later, under arrest, back to Caiaphas's house.

KEY SAYING

'Father, if you are willing, take this cup from me; yet not my will, but yours be done.'

LUKE 22:42

Peter, James, and John

Jesus formed a special friendship with Peter, James and John, who had been business partners long before Jesus called them (Luke 5:1–10) and so already had strong friendships. On five occasions in Mark we find Jesus with just these three: the healing of Peter's mother-in-law (Mark 1:29–31), the raising of Jairus's daughter (Mark 5:37), the transfiguration (Mark 9:2–13), discussing Jerusalem's future (Mark 13:3–4), and in Gethsemane (Mark 14:33). Why did Jesus take just these at times? Perhaps because he saw the potential within them; or perhaps because of something far more fundamental: the need for close friends with whom he could share his heart. Even among these three, there was an even closer friendship with John, 'the disciple whom Jesus loved' (e.g. John 13:23).

His Final Hours

ON TRIAL

After praying in Gethsemane until the early hours of the morning, Jesus was arrested and led off to face a series of trials that went through the night and into the next morning, leaving him without sleep. These twelve hours would be the final ones of his life. And yet the message that came through was that, strangely, it wasn't his opponents who were in control, but him.

The Sanhedrin

The Sanhedrin, the main religious, political and legal council in Jerusalem, comprised seventy-one members (reflecting Moses with his seventy elders), drawn from chief priests, scribes and elders, and presided over by the high priest. Their rules required trials to be conducted during daylight hours, to begin with the evidence for acquittal, and not to be held on days preceding a Sabbath or a festival. All these rules were ignored in the case of Jesus.

Caiaphas

According to Josephus, Caiaphas was high priest for eighteen years, taking office after the Romans deposed Annas, his father-in-law (though Annas remained a power-behind-the-throne). Caiaphas strongly opposed Jesus, telling his fellow-leaders after the raising of Lazarus, 'You do not realise that it is better for you that one man die for the people than that the whole nation perish' (John 11:50). For him this was a political comment, but John says he was prophesying more than he understood (11:51–52). He took the lead in getting rid of Jesus; and even after Jesus' death, his antagonism to Christians continued for many years (e.g. Acts 4:6–7).

FINAL JOURNEYS

1. Arrested in Gethsemane (Matthew 26:47–56; Mark 14:43–52; Luke 22:47–53; John 18:1–11).

2. Preliminary investigation by Annas, the former high priest (John 18:12–13, 19–24).

3. Questioned by Caiaphas, the high priest, to find evidence for use later before the Sanhedrin, the Jewish ruling council (Luke 22:54, 63–65).

4. Appearance before the Sanhedrin (Matthew 26:57 – 27:1; Mark 14:53 – 15:1; Luke 22:66–71). They questioned Jesus about his opposition to the Temple, especially his comments that he could destroy it and rebuild it in three days; but the witnesses couldn't agree on what he said. Caiaphas changed tack, questioning Jesus under oath, demanding to know whether he was the Messiah. With his messiahship no longer in danger of being misunderstood, Jesus finally acknowledged he was indeed Messiah, adding, 'You will see the Son of Man sitting at the right hand of the Mighty One and coming on the clouds of heaven' (Matthew 26:64). Caiaphas was delighted, his charge of blasphemy now clearly acknowledged by Jesus. Meanwhile Peter, outside in the courtyard, denied Jesus three times, just as Jesus prophesied (Luke 22:54–65; John 18:15–18, 25–27).

5. Appearance before Pilate, the Roman governor, who alone could impose the death penalty. The religious leaders now gave their accusations a political spin, accusing Jesus of opposing taxes to Caesar and claiming to be King of the Jews (Matthew 27:2, 11–14; Mark 15:1–5; Luke 23:1–5; John 18:28–40). Pilate found no basis for a charge (Luke 23:4) and, discovering he was Galilean, sent him to Herod.

6. Appearance before Herod Antipas, who ridiculed and mocked him (Luke 23:6–12). Jesus refused to answer any of his questions, so he returned him to Pilate.

7. Trial before Pilate, with demands for the death penalty (Matthew 27:15–26; Mark 15:6–15; Luke 23:13–25; John 18:39 – 19:16). His wife's dream about Jesus (Matthew 27:19) disturbed Pilate enough to try to release Jesus as part of the traditional Passover amnesty; but the leaders stirred up the crowds in favour of Barabbas, reminding Pilate that to release Jesus meant being 'no friend of Caesar' (John 19:12). Pilate washed his hands of the case, claiming he was innocent of Jesus' blood and that his death was their responsibility. With that, he handed him over for execution.

8. Roman soldiers mockingly dressed Jesus as a king, with a purple robe and crown of thorns, and then flogged him (Matthew 27:27–31; Mark 15:16–20).

9. Made to carry his cross to his place of execution, Jesus had no strength to continue, and Simon of Cyrene was forced by the soldiers to carry it for him (Matthew 27:32; Mark 15:21; Luke 23:26).

10. Crucifixion outside the city between two criminals (Matthew 27:33–56; Mark 15:22–41; Luke 23:32–49; John 19:17–37).

'This is your hour – when darkness reigns.'
LUKE 22:53

● SEE ALSO
CRUCIFIXION P. 102
HEROD P. 93
HIS OPPONENTS PP. 92–93

(Map of Jerusalem at the time of Jesus)

- 300 meters / 1000 feet (scale)
- Solomon's quarries
- Damascus Gate
- Tower Gate
- Pools of Bethesda
- Antonia Fortress
- Porticoes
- Shushan Gate
- Temple Mount
- The Temple
- Golden Gate
- Golgotha
- Warren's Gate
- Wilson's Arch
- Garden of Gethsemane
- Jaffa Gate
- ...ael Tower
- Hippicus Tower
- Mariamne Tower
- Barclay's Gate
- Solomon's Portico
- Pinnacle of the Temple
- Hasmonean Palace (Palace of Herod Antipas?)
- Robinson's Arch
- Herod's Palace
- Dung Gate
- Hulda Gates
- Single Gate
- Upper City
- Valley Gate
- Cheesemaker's Valley
- Kidron Valley
- Zion Gate
- Lower City
- House of Caiaphas?
- Hezekiah's Tunnel
- House of Annas?
- Essene Quarter
- ...ssene Gate
- Pool of Siloam
- Water Gate
- Ilinnom Valley
- Iekoa Gate

Legend:
- Area of the city at time of Jesus
- City Wall
- Modern City Wall

Pilate

This is an inscription from Caesarea's Roman theatre, naming Pontius Pilate as Prefect of Judea.

Appointed by Tiberius, Pilate was prefect from AD 26 to 36. Josephus and Philo describe him as hot-tempered and indifferent to the people he governed. For example, on arriving in Jerusalem he set up Roman standards with their figures of the emperor, immediately offending Jewish sensibilities; he later seized Temple funds to build an aqueduct, leading to riots and thousands of deaths; and Luke says he killed Galileans while sacrificing in the Temple, mixing their blood with that of their sacrifices (Luke 13:1). After the annihilation of a Samaritan mob, he was finally recalled to Rome where he disappeared into obscurity.

A Roman *flagrum* of the kind used on Jesus. Its leather thongs were knotted with metal or bone to inflict maximum damage on the victim.

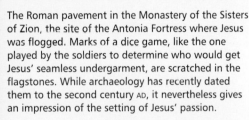

The Roman pavement in the Monastery of the Sisters of Zion, the site of the Antonia Fortress where Jesus was flogged. Marks of a dice game, like the one played by the soldiers to determine who would get Jesus' seamless undergarment, are scratched in the flagstones. While archaeology has recently dated them to the second century AD, it nevertheless gives an impression of the setting of Jesus' passion.

KEY SAYING

'It is written: "I will strike the shepherd, and the sheep will be scattered."'

MARK 14:27

His Crucifixion
THE DEATH OF GOD

While films often make great play of Jesus' sufferings, the Gospels are surprisingly reticent about them. The whole horror is summed up in short and simple words: 'And they crucified him' (Mark 15:24), just three words in the original Greek. The story of the past three years seemed, at last, to be over. The man who claimed to be God was dead.

His Execution

After his trials, Jesus was taken outside the city and was crucified between two common criminals (Matthew 27:32–56; Mark 15:21–40; Luke 23:26–49; John 19:16–37). A sign (the *titulus*) was nailed above his head recording his crime in Aramaic, Latin and Greek: 'This is the King of the Jews'. The religious leaders objected, wanting it changed to show this was a claim, not a reality, but Pilate refused. The crowds mocked Jesus, but even in his agony he prayed for their forgiveness. This was his darkest moment, even crying out, 'My God, my God, why have you forsaken me?' such was his sense of abandonment because of the sin he was carrying. The agony that could normally last days was over in a matter of hours. Suddenly he cried out one last time: 'It is finished!' (John 19:30). His work completed, he gave up his life and entrusted himself to his heavenly Father, as his earthly mother stood by, enduring an agony of her own.

Crucifixion

Crucifixion, which probably had Phoenician origins, was adopted by the Romans as a brutal means of execution to instil fear. The condemned man was flogged and made to carry the crossbar to the place of execution. Stripped naked, his wrists were nailed to the crossbar, which was lifted onto a stake fixed in the ground; his legs were pushed up and sideways and his ankles nailed to the upright so his arms had to carry his weight. Death came slowly, as the hanging body put huge strain on the diaphragm, making breathing almost impossible. Prisoners could remain conscious for days, and soldiers sometimes shortened their suffering by breaking their legs with iron clubs so they could no longer push up to get breath. The corpses were usually left for birds of prey.

Christ on the Cross by Diego Velazquez, c. 1630.

Ensuring His Death

The Jewish leaders wanted a speedy death to ensure Jesus wasn't left on the cross for Sabbath the next day (a measure of their religious hypocrisy). So they asked Pilate for his legs to be broken to hasten his death by preventing him pushing up on them to get respite for his breathing; but when the soldiers went to do this, they found Jesus already dead. To make sure, however, they thrust a spear into his body, blood and water spurting out (John 19:31–37). John couldn't have understood the significance of what he wrote, but what he was witnessing was the rupture of Jesus' heart.

Fulfilling Scripture

By anyone's standards, Jesus' life had been remarkable; but even more remarkable was how that life, and death, fulfilled prophecies written hundreds of years earlier. While some have suggested that Jesus 'set things up', consciously acting to fulfil Scripture so he could claim to be the Messiah, the sheer number of Old Testament prophecies he fulfilled makes such a view untenable. Rather, here was a man whose life and death had truly been foreseen.

What is remarkable is how some of those prophecies described his crucifixion down to minute details (e.g. Psalm 22:16–18, written 1,000 years earlier) and foresaw what he was doing through that death: paying the price of humanity's sin (e.g. Isaiah 52:13 – 53:12).

COMMENTS ON CRUCIFIXION

'The cruellest and most disgusting penalty.'
Cicero

'The most pitiable of deaths.'
Josephus

The Significance of Crucifixion

For both Romans and Jews, crucifixion was a vile death. For Romans, it was reserved for the worst of offenders, especially rebels. For Jews, it was shameful not only because your nakedness was exposed (as would have happened with Jesus, for the soldiers shared his clothing), but because their Law said, 'Anyone who is hung on a tree is under God's curse' (Deuteronomy 21:23). When Jesus died on the cross, therefore, he experienced not just death, but a death despised by everyone.

'They brought Jesus to the place called Golgotha (which means The Place of the Skull)... and they crucified him' (Mark 15:22, 24).
This rocky escarpment is believed by some to be 'the place of the skull', partly because it looks as if it has eye sockets and a nose, but also because of the presence of a nearby ancient tomb.

An Outbreak of Signs

At the moment Jesus died, it was as if the earth itself cried out in pain at what had happened: the Temple curtain was ripped in two, the earth shook, rocks split, tombs broke open, and many dead saints came back to life (Matthew 27:51–53). Physically, these events were caused by an earthquake (Matthew 27:54), but spiritually, there was much more going on.

First, the Temple curtain separated the Most Holy Place, representing God's presence, from the rest of the Temple, and its ripping in two symbolized either that through Jesus' death the way to God was now open, or possibly that God had now abandoned the Temple, as Ezekiel had prophesied (Ezekiel chapters 10–11). Second, the raising of some dead believers – no stranger in itself than the raisings Jesus had done during his lifetime – was prophetic of what would happen at the End Time when Jesus returned: the faithful dead would rise to be with him forever, and here was a foretaste of that.

Little wonder the Roman centurion exclaimed, 'Surely he was the Son of God!' (Matthew 27:54).

KEY SAYING

'Father, forgive them, for they do not know what they are doing.'
LUKE 23:34

His Burial

THE END OF THE JOURNEY

His death had been shameful enough, but an admirer of Jesus – or was he even a secret disciple by this point? – resolved that his body would not be shamed any further. Joseph of Arimathea took the body from the cross, wrapped it in linen and placed it in a nearby tomb. That, sadly, was the end of Jesus' journey; at least, that's what everybody thought.

A Kind Deed

Late on Friday afternoon, Joseph of Arimathea, a member of the Jewish Council who hadn't agreed to Jesus' death, took courage and asked Pilate for permission to give him a decent burial, rather than leaving him for birds of prey as was the Roman custom. Removing the body from the cross – not an easy task, for ossuaries from the time show that hands and feet sometimes had to be cut off to get the body down – he wrapped it in linen and took it to his own nearby tomb cut into the rock, which had never been used before. A heavy rolling-stone was then heaved across the entrance. Only John tells us he was accompanied by Nicodemus, another member of the Council, who had visited Jesus at night long before (John 3:1–21).

The women disciples followed them, watching at a distance before returning home to prepare spices for anointing the body. But the Sabbath, the day of rest, was now upon them, so that would have to wait till Sunday.

First-Century Burial Practices

Pictured here is the entrance to a first-century tomb near Jerusalem showing the rolling stone in place. A chamber was cut from the rock, from which shafts (*kohkim*) were dug further into the rock for burial places. Bodies were anointed with spices and wrapped in linen before being placed on a stone slab in the first chamber, which explains why John could look into the tomb on Sunday morning and immediately see that the body had gone (John 20:3–8). The entrances were low so that a rolling stone of manageable size could be placed across the entrance. Once the body had decomposed (which could take up to two years in Israel's dry climate), the bones were gathered together and placed in a stone box known as an ossuary.

THE GARDEN TOMB

The Garden Tomb in Jerusalem which, although probably not the original tomb of Jesus, is certainly like the one that was used. A large millstone, set in the channel which can still be seen, was rolled across the entrance to keep out scavenging animals and grave robbers (Matthew 27:57–60; Mark 15:42–47; Luke 23:50–53; John 19:38–42). The large stone bricks were added at the time of its discovery by General Gordon in 1867.

> *Joseph took the body, wrapped it in a clean linen cloth, and placed it in his own new tomb that he had cut out of the rock. He rolled a big stone in front of the entrance to the tomb and went away.*
> MATTHEW 27:59–60

The Church of the Holy Sepulchre

Seen here is the tomb of Jesus in the Church of the Holy Sepulchre (or 'Church of the Resurrection' to Eastern Orthodox Christians). This church claims to mark the sites of both Jesus' execution and burial and has a long tradition associated with it, a church being here for over 1,700 years. The alternative site, the Garden Tomb, wasn't identified until the nineteenth century.

Inside the church is a rocky outcrop, claimed to be the site of the crucifixion. Archaeology has shown this lay outside the city walls in Jesus' time, close to a gate, so it would have been ideal for crucifixions. Another part of the church preserves the claimed location of his tomb. Since other first-century tombs are preserved here, this was obviously a burial ground, so may well have been the location of Jesus' actual tomb.

His Burial in the Christian Message

'For what I received I passed on to you as of first importance: that Christ died for our sins according to the Scriptures, that he was buried, that he was raised on the third day according to the Scriptures' (1 Corinthians 15:3–4).

Paul's repetition of this creed that he received from others shows that the burial of Jesus was part of the earliest Christian message (see also Acts 13:27–29). It is as if the first Christians wanted us to know that there was no doubt whatsoever about Jesus' death, and therefore challenge us to consider why the tomb was empty three days later.

Good Friday

In English, the day Jesus died is called 'Good Friday', though the origin of this name is uncertain. It may have been because its outcome was seen to be 'good' for us, or because it was originally called 'God's Friday'. In other languages it has different names, however, such as Holy Friday. It is traditionally seen as a day of mourning when believers meditate on Jesus' sufferings and death and what that means. In some countries there are also processions or re-enactments of the day's events.

STATIONS OF THE CROSS

The Stations of the Cross, also known as Via Dolorosa ('The Way of Sorrows'), depict the final hours of Jesus' life. It is often followed by Roman Catholics on Good Friday or on an earlier Friday in Lent to enable them to meditate on the key scenes of Jesus' sufferings and death. The 'stations' are usually a series of fourteen pictures or sculptures depicting scenes from Jesus' condemnation through to his burial. This scene shows Jesus being laid in the tomb.

KEY SAYING

'I tell you the truth, unless a grain of wheat falls to the ground and dies, it remains only a single seed. But if it dies, it produces many seeds.'
JOHN 12:24

His Resurrection: Sunday
DEATH DEFEATED

It is hard to imagine the anguish felt by the women who went to Jesus' tomb on Sunday morning and found his body gone. As if his enemies hadn't caused him enough indignity, and now this. But suddenly, there he was, appearing first to Mary, then to ones and twos, then to groups. The impossible had happened, just as Jesus had said it would, though no one had understood him. The tomb couldn't hold him; he had risen from the dead.

The Empty Tomb

The priests had convinced Pilate to post guards and seal the tomb (Matthew 27:62–66), but that didn't stop an angel rolling back the stone (Matthew 28:2) – though he did so, not to let Jesus out, but to let the disciples in. Jesus had already gone, and the angel's invitation to the women was to look for themselves and see (Matthew 28:6). Jesus had passed through the grave-clothes and rock walls as easily as he would pass through the walls of the Upper Room later that day (John 20:19). The rolled-back stone was simply the first step in a process of convincing his disciples that he had indeed risen.

Sunday Morning

All four Gospels describe how women went to Jesus' tomb early on Sunday morning, having rested on the Sabbath, to finish burying Jesus properly but found it empty (Matthew 28:1–8; Mark 16:1–5; Luke 24:1–3; John 20:1–2). Their first thought was that someone had moved the body, so they ran to tell the disciples, and Peter and John went to investigate. It was to Mary Magdalene, however, left behind in the garden, that Jesus first appeared (John 20:10–18). At first she didn't recognize him, mistaking him for the gardener, until Jesus spoke her name. She ran to tell the others, who understandably didn't believe her. But later that day he appeared to Peter (Luke 24:34; 1 Corinthians 15:5), then to two unnamed disciples (Luke 24:13–35), and finally to all of them that evening as they sat behind locked doors for fear of the Jewish leaders (John 20:19–23). Thomas wasn't there and wouldn't believe a word of it until a week later when Jesus appeared to him.

What is clear from this is that the disciples weren't gullible, waiting for the slightest thing to give them hope. Resurrection was the furthest thing from their minds; none of them believed it at first. But gradually the unthinkable proved true: Jesus had indeed risen from the dead.

In this nineteenth-century illustration for *Christian Doctrine for Families,* the women discover the empty tomb of Jesus.

The Emmaus Road

Later that day two disciples were walking down the road to nearby Emmaus when Jesus suddenly appeared (Luke 24:13–35). Like Mary, they didn't recognize him initially, despite talking at length about the weekend's events with him. It was only when he broke bread with them later that 'their eyes were opened and they recognized him, and he disappeared from their sight' (verse 31). Suddenly the burning their hearts had experienced while they had been talking with him all made sense, and they hurried back to Jerusalem to tell the others.

● See Also
HIS BURIAL PP. 104–105
HIS DESTINY PP. 54–55
HIS RESURRECTION P.106

Alternative Explanations

While the resurrection is probably one of the biggest stumbling blocks for people considering Christianity, alternative explanations for the empty tomb raise their own problems:

Alternative Explanations	Problem
Grave robbers stole the body.	Roman guards were there to prevent this.
Disciples stole the body to start rumours of resurrection.	Resurrection wasn't in their thinking; Roman guards were at the tomb.
The authorities removed the body to stop rumours of resurrection.	They could have produced the body when claims of resurrection started.
The women went to the wrong tomb.	The authorities could have produced the body from the right tomb.
Jesus didn't die but simply passed out and revived in the cool tomb.	The soldiers were convinced he was dead. How feasible was it, after such torture, to roll back the stone from inside, overcome the guards, walk to Jerusalem, and look like the glorious conqueror of death?

The Third Day

The Bible says that Jesus rose 'on the third day'. That seems strange to the modern way of counting, but in those days you included the day on which you started counting; so Friday, Saturday, Sunday made three days. But why the third day? Why not one day, one hour or even one moment after his death? One simple answer might be that three days is what Jesus had prophesied (Matthew 16:21; 17:23); but the number three was also significant in Judaism, since God had often demonstrated his power on the third day of an event, there being almost fifty examples of this in the Bible. So Jesus' resurrection on the third day was a way of showing that this was *God* at work.

So what did Jesus do between Friday and Sunday? While the Bible says little about this, Peter says he 'went and preached to the spirits in prison' (1 Peter 3:19–20). 'Imprisoned spirits' in Jewish apocalyptic literature usually refers to fallen angelic beings, so this would suggest that Jesus was declaring his victory to fallen spiritual beings, letting them know that they were truly defeated.

Easter and Sunday

Easter became the greatest annual festival in the church as Christians celebrated the resurrection. But there was also a weekly celebration of it, for from earliest times they moved their day of corporate worship to 'the first day of the week', Sunday (Acts 20:7; 1 Corinthians 16:2). To abandon the long-established tradition of the Sabbath (Saturday) shows how important the resurrection was to them, and all mainstream churches have followed this practice ever since.

Key Saying

'No-one takes [my life] from me, but I lay it down of my own accord. I have authority to lay it down and authority to take it up again.'

JOHN 10:18

107

His Resurrection: The 39 Days
PREPARING FOR DEPARTURE

Christianity began, not with the life of Jesus, and not even with his death, but with his resurrection. Had those claims of resurrection been confined just to that first Sunday, they could easily have been dismissed as mere hysteria or wishful thinking. But claims of Jesus' appearances continued for a further thirty-nine days, and then suddenly stopped, never to be claimed again in that way. Clearly, this was a unique period.

Resurrection Appearances

In the thirty-nine days following Easter Sunday Jesus continued to appear to his followers, not only convincing them of his resurrection, but teaching them about God's kingdom (Acts 1:3). He came and went over this period, rather than staying with them, preparing them for his departure. Some of those he appeared to included:

■ **Thomas** (John 20:24–29)
Thomas wasn't there when Jesus appeared to the disciples and refused to believe them. One week later Jesus appeared to him (John 20:26–29), inviting him to do what he'd said would alone convince him: put his fingers in his wounds to prove it was him. Thomas fell on his knees, saying what Christians have acknowledged ever since: 'My Lord and my God!' (verse 28).

■ **A group of 500** (1 Corinthians 15:6)
Paul's list of resurrection witnesses in 1 Corinthians 15:3–8 is one of the earliest we have. He notes that Jesus 'appeared to more than five hundred of the brothers at the same time, most of whom are still living' (verse 6), the implication being they could therefore still be questioned by doubters.

■ **James** (1 Corinthians 15:7)
Listed separately to the apostles, this James was the brother of Jesus (Matthew 13:55), who didn't believe before the resurrection (John 7:5) but eventually became a leader in the Jerusalem church (Acts 15:13).

■ **Disciples by the lake** (John 21:1–14)
Jesus appeared to disciples who had been fishing all night but who, despite their experience, had caught nothing. Jesus called to them to cast their net on the other side, and they took one of their biggest catches ever: 153 large fish. Peter suddenly realized that the stranger on the beach was Jesus and leapt into the water, leaving the others to bring the catch.

Stained glass window from the Basilica of Saint Thomas in Chennai Tamil, India, depicts Jesus with his disciples.

PETER'S RESTORATION

The Church of Peter's Primacy, built around the rock from which, according to tradition, Jesus directed his disciples to catch fish (John 21:1–14). Here Jesus restored Peter, letting him cancel his threefold denial (Matthew 26:69–75) with a threefold declaration of love (John 21:15–19), and commissioning him for his future work.

He appeared to them over a period of forty days and spoke about the kingdom of God.
ACTS 1:3

● SEE ALSO
HIS DESTINY PP. 54–55
HIS MESSAGE P.115
RESURRECTION PP. 106–107

THE RESURRECTION BODY

While recognizably human (walking, talking, eating), Jesus' post-resurrection body was also different. Even his closest friends didn't recognize him immediately; Mary thought he was the gardener until he spoke her name; the disciples on the Emmaus Road thought he was another traveller until he broke bread. Something had clearly happened to his body.

Paul wrote about 'the resurrection body' (1 Corinthians 15:35–57), explaining how God gives his people a 'spiritual body' (verse 44) suitable for life in the new age, just as he gives creatures bodies suitable for their realm of life. God won't leave us as incorporeal spirits but will transform us with new 'spiritual bodies' suitable for the new creation, just like caterpillars are gloriously transformed into butterflies.

Noli me Tangere, c. 1491, by Sandro Botticelli.

The Nazareth Inscription

A marble tablet, dating from shortly after the resurrection, conveys Caesar's edict forbidding interference with tombs, on pain of death. It may simply have been a prohibition against tomb robbery; but why was it issued in obscure Nazareth, rather than key cities? Was it because news of the disappearance of Jesus of Nazareth's body and claims of resurrection had reached the Roman authorities and they wanted to quell any further such stories?

What Was the Point?

If the resurrection really happened, as Christians claim, what was its point?

■ It confirmed Jesus as the Messiah who had indeed brought God's kingdom and whose resurrection confirmed the promised new age was breaking in.

■ It showed that Jesus wasn't just a prophet but the Lord of life, proving it by conquering death.

■ It meant that death wasn't the end for Jesus' followers, for what had happened to him would happen to them.

■ It was God's confirmation of Jesus' promise that he had indeed come to 'give his life as a ransom for many' (Matthew 20:28).

The Ascension

Forty days after the resurrection (Acts 1:3), Jesus took his disciples near to Bethany where he 'ascended' to heaven (Luke 24:50–52; Acts 1:1–11), enveloped as he went by a cloud, symbolizing (as in the Old Testament) God's presence. It was as if his Father had come to take him home. The disciples just stared, unable to believe their eyes, and it took two angels to jolt them into action.

The ascension was about Jesus returning to his proper place at God's right hand. The amazing thing, however, is that he returned different from how he came: he took his humanity with him.

The ascension convinced Christians that Jesus was exalted in heaven, reigning over his enemies (Acts 2:32–33; 5:30–31; Ephesians 4:7–10; Colossians 1:2; Hebrews 4:14; 1 Peter 3:22). Revelation in particular, written at a time of persecution, boldly declares that, despite the worst the devil can do, Jesus is still reigning on his throne (Revelation 1:12–18; 5:1–10; 7:9–17).

The Great Commission

Before his ascension, Jesus gave his followers one final instruction, which Christians call the great commission: to take his message into the whole world (Matthew 28:18–20; Acts 1:8). His own ministry had been confined to Israel, but now the message could go further, inviting all nations to become part of his 'new Israel'.

KEY SAYING

'Because you have seen me, you have believed; blessed are those who have not seen and yet have believed.'

JOHN 20:29

His Apostles

MEN WITH A MISSION

From among his many followers Jesus had chosen twelve to be his 'apostles' ('messengers') and had sent them out to preach the message of God's kingdom (Mark 3:13–19). Now, before returning to his Father, he had repeated that commission: but this time the task wasn't just to go to Israel, but to the whole world (Matthew 28:18–20; Acts 1:8). Before they could do that, however, they had to wait. Something was missing.

Transformation at Pentecost

It was 9 a.m. and the disciples were waiting to start celebrating Pentecost. Suddenly, what seemed like wind and fire rushed in, and they were filled with the Holy Spirit and began to speak in tongues (Acts 2:1–4). This experience led bystanders to think they were drunk; but Peter explained what had happened, how it fulfilled Joel's prophecy, and how this was the Holy Spirit that the crucified, risen and now exalted Jesus had sent, just as he promised (Acts 2:16–39). Three thousand responded to his message and were baptized that day (verse 41). The mission Jesus had given them had exploded into being.

WHERE IT HAPPENED

While it is often assumed the Spirit came in the Upper Room, Acts doesn't actually say this. In fact, it's more likely to have happened in the Temple. In support of this:

■ The disciples numbered 120 (Acts 1:15), too many for a house, but easily accommodated in the Temple's courtyard.

■ They attracted a huge crowd (Acts 2:6), understandable in the Temple, impossible in Jerusalem's narrow streets.

■ The new converts were baptized immediately (Acts 2:40–41), easy to do in the Temple's ritual baths.

■ The wind 'filled the whole house' (Acts 2:2), and the Temple was often called God's 'house'.

■ Temple attendance at Pentecost was mandatory for Jewish men, so the disciples are highly likely to have gone there, despite their fear. With thousands crowding the city, it wouldn't have been difficult to escape notice.

Jesus' choice of this very public location underlined from the beginning that the gift of the Spirit was for empowering his followers to proclaim his message.

Days of Waiting

After Jesus' ascension, the disciples returned to Jerusalem and didn't know what else to do but pray. They sensed the need to replace Judas, who had committed suicide (Matthew 27:1–10; Acts 1:18–19), to bring their number back to twelve (paralleling the twelve patriarchs of ancient Israel) as the foundation of the 'new Israel' Jesus was building. Not having Jesus to ask, they resorted to the only way they knew of getting God's guidance: they 'cast lots' between two candidates who were both eyewitnesses of Jesus' life, death and resurrection (Acts 1:21–26). Matthias's name came up, 'so he was added to the eleven apostles'.

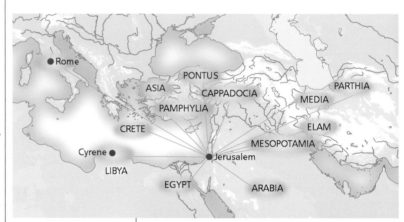

Peter's audience came from far and wide, as this map shows. As the converts returned home, they took the message with them, the first Christian missionaries.

The royal *stoa*, a large colonnaded area at the southern end of the Court of the Gentiles in the Temple, the likely location of the giving of the Spirit.

He appointed twelve – designating them apostles – that they might be with him and that he might send them out...

MARK 3:14

● SEE ALSO
HIS ASCENSION P. 109
HIS CHURCH PP. 112–113
HIS DISCIPLES PP. 34–35

WHY PENTECOST?

Pentecost was a particularly suitable time for the giving of the Spirit for it celebrated two things: the giving of the Law and the main harvest. Through the Spirit there was now both a new 'law', written on people's hearts just as the prophets had promised (Jeremiah 31:33; Ezekiel 36:26–27), and a new harvest, a harvest of people. Both would be key aspects of the Spirit's work.

Stephen's Martyrdom

Opposition to Jesus' apostles wasn't long in coming. Peter and John were arrested for healing someone (Acts 3:1 – 4:21); the whole group was arrested and told not to preach about Jesus (Acts 5:17–42); even ordinary church members were persecuted (Acts 8:1–3). But Christianity's first martyr was Stephen (Acts 6:8 – 8:1). His miracles and wisdom antagonized the religious leaders, and he quickly found himself accused of blasphemy before Caiaphas, the high priest. Preaching boldly, he challenged what they had done to Jesus; but when he had a vision of Jesus, claiming to see him standing alongside God, it was the ultimate blasphemy for them and they stoned him to death.

While Stephen was the first Christian martyr, he wasn't the last. Peter and Paul both followed him in due course, as have countless Christians throughout the ages and still today. The intriguing question is: why do some want to kill Christians for their beliefs, and what makes Christians ready to pay that ultimate price?

Paul Meets Jesus

Paul, an ardent opponent of Christianity (Acts 8:1–3), knew that if it reached Damascus on the key trade routes, then it could spread everywhere; so he resolved to stop it. Backed by the Sanhedrin, he sought out Christians, taking them back to Jerusalem (Acts 9:1–2). What he hadn't counted on, however, was meeting the very man whose message he opposed. Blinded by a light on the Damascus Road, Paul heard a voice asking why he was persecuting him. When he asked who it was, the voice replied, 'I am Jesus, whom you are persecuting' (Acts 9:5). Still blinded, he continued to Damascus where he was prayed for by Ananias, a Christian. He immediately regained his sight, was filled with the Holy Spirit and was baptized as a follower of Jesus (Acts 9:17–19). He later insisted that this experience (around AD 35) wasn't just a vision, but an actual encounter with the risen Jesus (1 Corinthians 9:1; 15:8) that dramatically re-orientated his life and turned him from arch-persecutor to arch-promoter of Christianity, raising him to the ranks of the apostles.

KEY SAYING

'Do not leave Jerusalem, but wait for the gift my Father promised, which you have heard me speak about... in a few days you will be baptised with the Holy Spirit.'

ACTS 1:4–5

111

His Church

GOD'S NEW PEOPLE

After Pentecost, the new community that Jesus had come to establish – variously called 'followers of the Way' (Acts 9:1–2), 'the believers' (Acts 2:44), 'the church' (Acts 8:1–3) – suddenly surged ahead. While perhaps too strong to say that Pentecost was its birth-day (after all, Jesus started to build this community while here on earth), it was certainly its launch-day. Empowered by the Spirit, the church now started to live out everything Jesus had prepared them for, pushing out beyond Israel. Within a generation they would be found in every key city in the Roman empire.

Added In

While Jesus said faith needed to be personal, he never intended it to be private. Faith that draws people closer to God inevitably draws them closer to one another, as Jesus had modelled with his disciples. All who responded to Jesus in repentance and faith, Peter said in his Pentecost sermon, could receive God's Spirit, just like them, and become part of the 'new Israel' that Jesus' death and resurrection had made possible (Acts 2:38–39). Those who responded weren't left isolated but 'were added to their number' (Acts 2:41), becoming part of this 'new Israel', the church. In New Testament thinking, it is impossible to be a follower of Jesus without being part of his church.

Early Church Life

The post-Pentecost church was vibrant and relational. Acts 2:42–47 reveals its key features:

■ Use of homes for meetings (verse 46; see also 5:42)

■ A focus on teaching, fellowship, breaking bread and prayer (verse 42)

■ An atmosphere of the miraculous (verse 43)

■ Generosity with possessions (verses 44–45; see also 4:32–36)

■ Joy (verses 46–47)

■ People added to their number daily (verse 47)

In short, it was a continuation of the life that Jesus had modelled while among them. These characteristics continued throughout Acts, though Luke is honest enough to show that church life wasn't always perfect and that it had its problems at times (e.g. Acts 5:1–11; 15:36–41).

Church is People

Nowadays we tend to use the word 'church' to mean a religious building ('Let's go to church'), and they come in all sorts of shapes and sizes; but that's not how Jesus or the New Testament used it. For them 'church' always meant the people, never the place. Indeed church buildings didn't develop until after the emperor Constantine's conversion in AD 312 and his legalization of Christianity the following year. This was something of a two-edged sword, however. While it spared Christianity cruel persecution, it also turned it into a state religion, with church buildings springing up and church structures developing on imperial lines, leading at times to more of a focus on these things than the people they were meant to serve.

They gathered the church together.
ACTS 14:27

● SEE ALSO
HOLY COMMUNION PP. 96-97
JESUS' BAPTISM P. 30
THE NEW COMMUNITY, PP. 56–57

Images of the Church

The New Testament uses a number of different images to describe the church, each bringing out a different aspect of the character or purpose for which Jesus established it:

■ Bride (e.g. Revelation 21:2, 9; Ephesians 5:25–33)

■ Family or household (e.g. 1 Timothy 3:15; Hebrews 2:11)

■ God's house (e.g. Hebrews 3:6)

■ Temple (e.g. 1 Corinthians 3:16; Ephesians 2:19–22)

■ People (e.g. 1 Peter 2:9–10; Revelation 7:9)

■ Priesthood (e.g. 1 Peter 2:4–5, 9–10; Revelation 5:9–10)

■ Flock (e.g. Acts 20:28; 1 Peter 5:2)

■ Body (e.g. Romans 12:4–5; 1 Corinthians 12:27)

BAPTISM

Just as circumcision had been the outward sign of relationship with God in the Old Testament, so baptism became that outward sign in the New Testament. Jesus himself had led the way by being baptized (Matthew 3:13–17; Mark 1:9–11; Luke 3:21–22; John 1:29–34), and his final command to his disciples was to preach the gospel and baptize those who believed (Matthew 28:19). Churches today differ in their practice of baptism. Some believe it should

only be for those who have made a conscious decision to follow Jesus, stressing there are no examples of infant baptism (or 'christening') in the New Testament and that baptizing babies sends the wrong idea of what it means to be a Christian. Others, however, basing their practice more on post-apostolic church tradition than New Testament evidence, baptize the infants of believers, seeing it as a parallel to circumcision in the Old Testament.

Early Struggles

The early church didn't always find it easy to follow Jesus' teaching. The *idea* of loving one another is easy; but how did Christians from Jewish backgrounds, for whom ritual hand-washings and keeping the Sabbath had always been so important, actually live with Christians from Gentile backgrounds for whom these things seemed stupid? How could they even eat together without everybody feeling uncomfortable? And the problem got bigger, not smaller, as the church began to realize that Jesus had meant what he said when he told them to 'make disciples of *all* nations' (Matthew 28:19). Not everybody was comfortable with the gospel embracing Gentiles, at least without them having to embrace Jewish practices, and it wasn't long before Peter found his actions being challenged (Acts 11:1–3) and Paul found opponents dogging his footsteps (Galatians 2:11–21). The issue was finally resolved at the Council of Jerusalem in AD 50 (Acts 15:1–35), when the apostles and elders met to listen to both sides of the argument. It was James who finally proposed a solution that everyone accepted, which involved everyone having to learn to change, but also removing unnecessary obstacles to fellowship together.

Christians

'The disciples were called Christians first at Antioch' (Acts 11:26).

The term 'Christians' ('Christ-people') was probably originally a nickname given to followers of Jesus by others; however, it quickly became the name they adopted for themselves. It underlined that being a Christian was not about belonging to a particular group, family or church, but rather being someone who has personally chosen to follow Jesus Christ.

KEY SAYING

'I will build my church, and the gates of Hades will not overcome it.'

MATTHEW 16:18

113

His Mission
THE MESSAGE SPREADS

Despite fierce opposition, nothing could stop the ongoing mission of Jesus. At first his followers' greatest problem was the Jewish authorities, who opposed their claims about him, persecuting and killing them for it; but as the gospel reached the Gentile world, they came face to face not just with other competing religions but with the might of the Roman emperor, who was claiming divinity and who rejected any claim that 'Jesus is Lord', for he alone was Lord. And yet, despite all this, the message kept spreading.

PAUL'S TRAVELS

Perhaps more than any other individual it was Paul who was responsible for taking the gospel beyond the confines of Palestine. The map below shows his four missionary journeys, each time pushing beyond the previous boundary, and experiencing many trials along the way (2 Corinthians 6:3–10; 11:23–29). He ended up in Rome under house arrest for two years awaiting his hearing before Caesar (Acts 28:30–31). His letters reveal that he was released and returned to his mission, possibly even reaching Spain; but his final words show him back in prison again, this time awaiting the death penalty (2 Timothy 4:6–8). He was martyred around AD 67, probably, as a Roman citizen, by being beheaded.

Rapid Expansion

The church expanded rapidly in the thirty years following the resurrection, going way beyond its Jewish roots. Beginning with the conversion of Samaritans (Acts 8:4–25), seen as 'half-Jews', then reaching a eunuch (Acts 8:26–38), whose condition meant he could never become a Jew, then a Roman centurion and his household (Acts 10:1–48), it finally broke through to Gentiles in Antioch (Acts 11:19–21) from where Paul took it across Asia Minor to Greece and Rome (Acts 13:1 – 28:31). Jesus' promise to his followers that they would take his message to the whole world came true, and people of every racial or social background were included.

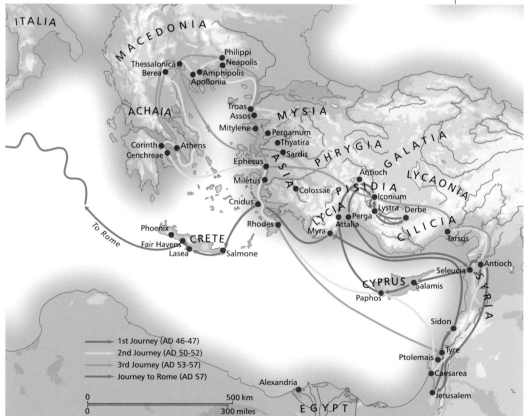

Map legend:
- 1st Journey (AD 46-47)
- 2nd Journey (AD 50-52)
- 3rd Journey (AD 53-57)
- Journey to Rome (AD 57)

| 0 | | 500 km |
| 0 | | 300 miles |

While Acts focuses on Christianity's spread across the Roman world, it was also spreading in other directions. Early Christian tradition says that Thomas went to India and Matthew to Ethiopia and Arabia. This is a priest of the Syrian Mar Thoma Church in Kerala, south India, which claims roots going back to Thomas.

Do not be ashamed to testify about our Lord.
2 Timothy 1:8

Opposition

As they undertook their mission, the apostles faced opposition, just as Jesus said they would (John 15:18–25).

- **Peter and John:** arrested for healing someone (Acts 3:1 – 4:21)

- **The twelve:** arrested and told not to speak about Jesus (Acts 5:17–42)

- **Stephen:** arrested for blasphemy and stoned to death (Acts 6:8 – 7:60)

- **The Jerusalem church:** persecuted (Acts 8:1–3)

- **James:** killed by Herod Agrippa (Acts 12:12)

- **Peter:** arrested by Herod but miraculously released (Acts 12:3–19)

- **Paul and Silas:** imprisoned for releasing a slave-girl from demons (Acts 16:16–39)

- **Paul:** arrested, tried and sent to Rome for Caesar's judgment (Acts 21:27 – 26:32)

- **John:** exiled to Patmos as a slave-labourer (Revelation 1:9)

Nero

In AD 64 much of Rome was destroyed by fire, reputedly started on the instructions of Nero, whose plans for remodelling the city had been blocked by the senate. Nero made Christians the scapegoat and thousands were crucified, thrown to lions, made to fight gladiators or set alight as human torches in his gardens. It was during this period that both Peter and Paul were martyred.

Pliny the Younger, a Roman governor writing to Emperor Trajan in AD 106, seeking advice on how to punish Christians, notes: *'They were accustomed to meeting on a fixed day before it was light, when they sang responsively a hymn to Christ as to a god, and bound themselves by solemn oath, not to any crime, but never to commit any fraud, theft, adultery, never to falsify their word, nor to refuse to return a trust... The contagion of this superstition has spread not only to the cities but also to the villages and farms.'*

Their Message

Some have accused Paul of taking Jesus' simple message ('love God, love your neighbour') and making it a complex religion, turning the message *of* Jesus into a message *about* Jesus. But this ignores what Jesus himself said was the heart of his message: the kingdom of God, a kingdom that was focused on *him. He* was the message, and the apostles simply drew out the implications of this in the light of the cross, resurrection and ascension. In particular they focused on two things:

1. Who Jesus was

The cross, resurrection and ascension convinced the church that Jesus wasn't just a rabbi or even just the Messiah, but the exalted Lord, no one less than God himself:

- 'The Son is the radiance of God's glory and the exact representation of his being...' (Hebrews 1:3)

- 'He is the image of the invisible God... by him all things were created' (Colossians 1:15–16)

- 'Christ, who is God over all' (Romans 9:5)

2. What Jesus did

Paul, as a former highly trained Jewish rabbi, quickly saw how Jesus fulfilled the Old Testament. In particular he saw that Jesus' death was directly linked to our forgiveness, interpreting that death as:

- **A sacrifice:** Jesus died in our place, as our substitute, so we could be cleansed (Romans 3:25; 5:6–7).

- **A redemption:** Jesus paid the price to free us from slavery to sin, as surely as Israel had been freed from slavery in Egypt (Romans 3:24; Ephesians 1:7–8).

- **A verdict:** we have received God's End Time 'not guilty' verdict right now, because Jesus paid for our sins and therefore no charge stands against us (Romans 3:21–26; 5:1–2; 8:1–2).

- **A reconciliation:** Jesus broke down the barriers separating us from God, one another and creation itself (Romans 5:9–11; Ephesians 2:14–22).

Key Saying

'You will receive power when the Holy Spirit comes upon you; and you will be my witnesses in Jerusalem, and in all Judea and Samaria, and to the ends of the earth.'

ACTS 1:8

His Influence

IMPACTING THE WORLD

As the mission that Jesus gave those first disciples has continued to grow through the past 2,000 years, his influence has been enormous. Every area of life – art, architecture, music, literature, education, law, politics, ethics, healthcare, social improvement – has been affected by his followers, whose faith has caused them to make a difference. This man has truly impacted the world.

Music

Christianity has inspired all kinds of music down the centuries – classical anthems, Gregorian plainchant, requiem masses, gospel, country and western, hymns, pop – as composers expressed their faith for their time and culture. One of the best-known pieces is the *Messiah*, composed by George Friedrich Handel (1685–1759), which is a magnificent portrayal of Jesus' life and significance.

Art

Probably no one in history has been painted more than Jesus, as artists through the ages have expressed his humanity and divinity, sufferings and glory. Some works, like those by Leonardo da Vinci, Raphael and Michelangelo, still stun today. Art would certainly have been the poorer had artists not created paintings, frescos, icons, sculptures and stained glass reflecting their vision of Jesus.

'Christ Pantocrator' ('Christ, ruler of everything'), was a common title from the fourth century after Constantine's conversion. Christ's right hand is raised in blessing while his left hand holds the New Testament. This example is from an icon at Aghiou Pavlou Monastery on Mount Athos.

Architecture

From the time Christians started having buildings of their own in the fourth century, architecture has portrayed their faith. But it was the rise of Gothic architecture in the twelfth century that gave churches their sense of grandeur. Flying buttresses made it possible to have higher walls and larger windows, with stained glass portraying Bible stories, and this height and light brought a new sense of God's majesty. Masons gave their whole lifetime to creating masterpieces, often hidden from view, prompted by their faith.

The interior of Chartres Cathedral, France, built in Gothic style with pointed arches and ribbed vaults.

Live as children of light.
EPHESIANS 5:8

SEE ALSO
HIS ETHICS PP. 68–69
LOVE P. 44
SERMON ON THE MOUNT PP. 46–47

Literature

Christianity has been a huge inspiration for poetry, fiction and drama, as well as more directly spiritual writings. The Gospels spawned a passion for writing about Jesus, and the Early Church Fathers were prolific in what they produced. Gutenberg's invention of the printing press (1450) led to an explosion of Christian literature, spurring on the Reformation. Some of the best-known Christian fiction includes Dante's *Divine Comedy* (1308–21), John Milton's *Paradise Lost* (1667), and John Bunyan's *Pilgrim's Progress* (1678).

Education

Christians have been hugely influential in the development of education. Monks provided simple teaching, and universities developed from religious orders providing education in Paris, Oxford and Cambridge, seeking to understand all of life in terms of its relationship to God. The Czech Jan Comenius (1592–1670), a Moravian, was one of the earliest champions of universal education, summed up in his book *Didactica Magna*, while Robert Raikes (1736–1811) pioneered Sunday schools in Britain, convinced that education was the best way of helping people out of poverty. Since children worked six days a week, his Sunday schools taught children to read, using the Bible as a textbook. Christians are still significantly involved in education throughout the world, especially in developing nations, where they are often the leading education providers.

Christian Values

Christian values are the essential basis of Western legal and ethical codes. Concepts like freedom, dignity, equality, forgiveness, tolerance, the value of the individual and the right to act according to conscience are fundamental liberties we would not enjoy today in the West had followers of Jesus not taken his principles and grafted them into the very fabric of society. Without Jesus and his influence, society would not have developed in the way it has.

The atheist's argument that religion has done more harm than good simply does not stand up to any honest investigation of history. While every religion has undoubtedly had its dark moments, it should not be forgotten that atheistic communism caused the deaths of 90 million people in the first half of the twentieth century. By contrast, Christianity still remains one of the most powerful forces for good in the world today.

Social Justice

Christians have often been at the forefront of fighting for social justice. Elizabeth Fry (1780–1845), a Quaker, horrified by the conditions of Newgate prison, started visiting women prisoners and founded a society for prison reform. Her work led to laws regulating prison conditions. Martin Luther King, Jr (1929–68)

played a leading role in the USA Civil Rights movement. He organized many non-violent protests, the best known being the Washington March (1963) supporting President Kennedy's Civil Rights bill, when he made his famous 'I have a dream' speech. Helder Camara (1909–99), a Roman Catholic archbishop (shown here), was a leading figure in Latin America's 'liberation theology' movement, strongly defending the rights of the poor through non-violent means and challenging the unjust structures that brought about their poverty.

Caring for the Poor

Albert Schweitzer (1875–1965), a renowned German theologian, philosopher, musician and missionary doctor, won the 1952 Nobel Peace Prize for his philosophy of 'Reverence for Life', expressed in many ways but most famously through his founding a hospital at his own expense in Lambaréné in French Equatorial Africa (Gabon). Mother Teresa (1910–97), an Albanian Roman Catholic nun, founded the Missionaries of Charity in Calcutta to care for India's poor, sick, orphaned and dying. By the time of her death the mission had 610 bases in 123 countries, with hospices, homes for AIDS and leprosy patients, soup kitchens, orphanages and schools.

William Wilberforce (1759–1833), whose Christian faith led him to devote his life to the abolition of slavery. After eighteen years of his tireless work as a British Member of Parliament, the Slave Trade Act was passed in 1807, banning slave trading. It was another twenty-six years before the Slavery Abolition Act was passed, freeing slaves throughout the British empire, one month after Wilberforce's death.

KEY SAYING

'You are the light of the world. A city on a hill cannot be hidden.'

MATTHEW 5:14

His Admirers
OTHER FAITHS AND JESUS

While a third of the world's population claims some sort of Christian allegiance, a significant number of those who don't still have huge respect for Jesus. By any standards he was a remarkable man; but people with any sort of spiritual awareness recognize there was something quite special about him. While they wouldn't agree with Christian claims for him, they nevertheless recognize there was something about Jesus that was unique. This in itself is amazing in our pluralistic society.

The Pluralist Religious Marketplace

There are now more choices than ever in the religious marketplace, so the church can no longer assume it is the representative of a common religious culture or common moral values that it once was. It has to sell its wares once again; and since this was what the first followers of Jesus had to do in exactly the same sort of pluralistic setting – and with considerable success – maybe that isn't such a bad thing.

Islam

Islam, the world's second-largest religion, acknowledges Jesus (Isa) as a great prophet who called people back to belief in the one true God. He is highly honoured in the Qur'an, Islam's holy book, where he is called 'Son of Mary', Messiah (no other prophet is called this in Islam), a spirit of God and word of God. However, while it says that he 'came unto them with clear proofs' (that is, miracles of healing and raising the dead), he remains 'no more than a Messenger', and his revelation is less than that of Muhammad, whom Muslims see as the last and greatest prophet and whose revelation from God, committed verbatim to the Qur'an, is final.

Points of similarity
There are many things about Jesus that Christians and Muslims agree on; for example:

- His virgin birth
- His sinlessness
- He was Messiah and Word of God
- He ascended to God's right hand
- He will come again

Points of difference
However, there are also significant points where the Qur'an conflicts with New Testament teaching about Jesus:

- **His incarnation:** Islam doesn't accept that Jesus was God, though it does accept his virgin birth. For Muslims, seeing Jesus as God's Son undermines God's unity and is a return to polytheism. 'God has no associates' is their cry. By contrast, the very heart of Christianity is that Jesus is no one less than God himself come into this world through his incarnation.

- **His death:** the Qur'an refers to Jesus' death but says, 'they killed him not, nor crucified him, but the resemblance of Isa was put over another man'. That is, God replaced Jesus with someone else on the cross in order to translate him to heaven, which contradicts the evidence of the Gospels.

- **His resurrection:** Islam understands Jesus' resurrection in terms of his translation to heaven: 'Allah took him up to himself.' Islam therefore removes the crucial point of Jesus' death and resurrection which lies at the heart of Christian faith.

- **His return:** the Qur'an itself doesn't mention Jesus' return before the final judgment, though it is found in many popular Islamic writings.

The Virgin Mary with the infant Jesus. Muslims share Christians' belief that Jesus was miraculously conceived by Mary while still a virgin.

'Could this be the Christ?'

JOHN 4:29

● SEE ALSO
HIS TEACHING ABOUT HIMSELF PP. 52–53
INCARNATION P. 24
TRINITY P. 25

Hinduism

Hinduism, the world's third-largest religion, is a diverse spirituality rooted in India's Vedic scriptures and embraces most expressions of religion. While Hindus believe there is ultimately only one God, this God finds expression in 33 million deities, which inevitably makes for a variety of stories, practices, festivals and sacrifices. Hinduism believes in reincarnation: at death the body dies but the soul lives on, adopting a new body. This continues, up or down life's ladder depending how we lived our previous life, until we reach *moksha* (liberation). By contrast, Christians believe in just one God and one life in this world.

Given Hinduism's variety of expressions, it can have a wide range of responses to Christianity. While some militants are extremely antagonistic towards Christians, seeing Christianity as a Western invasion of their culture, the very nature of Hinduism makes most Hindus receptive to Jesus and open to receiving prayer in his name, seeing him as the epitome of Hindu ideals. Many Indian Christians believe it is by demonstrating Jesus' power and care that they can show their fellow-countrymen that he is far more than just another guru.

Hindus ritually bathing to maintain their purity. For Christians, purity comes through the once-for-all sacrifice of Jesus on the cross.

Modern Spirituality

The second half of the twentieth century saw a huge increase of interest in spirituality of various kinds in the West as people reacted to intellectualism and scientific worldviews that had dominated thinking for so long. That spirituality found many expressions, with an explosion of new religions and spiritual movements, often characterized by believing without belonging and a focus on self rather than on others. Its growth has led many Westerners to being open to re-examining Jesus in a new way. Many 'New Age' philosophies respect Jesus and his teachings, though often struggle with the church – a challenge to those who belong to it.

Do All Paths Lead to God?

In our pluralistic world it is increasingly common to be told that all religions are the same and all lead to God in the end. However, while there are indeed similarities between the different religions, they offer very different visions of God, how to find him, how to please him, how to get right with him, what happens after death, to name but a few. The Christian response, however, stark though it sounds, cannot be less than that of Jesus who said, 'I am the way and the truth and the life. No-one comes to the Father except through me' (John 14:6).

His Hope
LIVING IN THE LIGHT OF ETERNITY

Is life getting better, or worse? The truth is, it's probably a mixture of both. We hear of great medical breakthroughs or amazing acts of courage and think how well mankind is doing; but then we hear of the latest crisis or some act of savagery and think what a long way mankind has still to go. Through all these ups and downs, however, what has spurred Christians on and kept them engaged in Jesus' mission is the hope he gave them for the future.

Jesus' Teaching

Many of Jesus' parables – the tenants, the wedding banquet, the servants, the ten virgins, the talents, the sheep and goats – spoke of future hope for his followers, as well as future judgment for those who rejected him. Jesus underlined this hope the night before his crucifixion when, sensing the disciples' anxiety, he assured them, 'In my Father's house are many rooms; if it were not so, I would have told you. I am going there to prepare a place for you. And if I go and prepare a place for you, I will come back and take you to be with me that you also may be where I am' (John 14:2–3). Jesus was confident, not only of his own destiny, but of that of all who believed in him.

Jesus' Return

Jesus said God's ultimate plan would climax on the day he returned to this world to destroy evil, judge sinners and establish God's new creation. While the New Testament contains no systematic teaching about that return, Jesus outlined four key elements of it in Mark 13:24–37 saying it would be:

- **Personal** (verse 26): his return isn't a metaphor for death, but a promise that he himself will come back, just as he left (see Acts 1:11).

- **Public** (verses 24–27): his return will not be secret but as public as a royal visit.

- **Triumphant** (verse 26): his return will not be quiet like his first coming, but glorious and victorious (see 1 Thessalonians 4:13–18).

- **Unexpected** (verses 32–37): life will be carrying on as normal when he will suddenly appear (Matthew 24:36–44), like a thief in the night (1 Thessalonians 5:2; 2 Peter 3:10).

While Christians often describe this return as 'the second coming', the New Testament never actually uses this term, but rather three Greek words:

'The Lord himself will come down from heaven, with a loud command, with the voice of the archangel and with the trumpet call of God, and the dead in Christ will rise first. After that, we who are still alive and are left will be caught up together with them in the clouds to meet the Lord in the air. And so we will be with the Lord for ever' (1 Thessalonians 4:16–17).

- ***Parousia*** = 'arrival' (James 5:7–8; 2 Peter 3:4). Used of public visits of emperors and kings when everyone in the city had to turn out to greet them.

- ***Apokalypsis*** = 'revelation' (Luke 17:30; 2 Thessalonians 1:7). Used of raising the curtain in theatres. Jesus' coming will 'lift the curtain' to show things as they really are.

- ***Epiphaneia*** = 'appearance' (2 Thessalonians 2:8; Titus 2:13). Literally, 'glorious manifestation', as Jesus is seen in all his glory.

Now the dwelling of God is with men, and he will live with them.
REVELATION 21:3

The Last Days

The Bible says that the end of history will be preceded by great troubles (e.g. Matthew 24:29; 2 Timothy 3:1–5), which is why Christians have often thought they were in 'the last days', especially during times of persecution or crisis. But actually the Bible sees *the whole period* between Jesus' ascension and return as 'the last days'. Rather than being an 'end' that we walk *towards*, 'the last days' are an end that we constantly walk *along*, like a cliff edge over which we could be pushed at any moment. That's why it's important to always be ready, Jesus said (Matthew 24:44).

While some things will characterize this whole 'last days' period – apostasy, false religion, godlessness, persecution, increasing catastrophes – the Bible prophesies the appearance of one final opponent immediately before Jesus' return called 'Antichrist' (1 John 2:18–22; 4:3; 2 John 7), 'the man of lawlessness' (2 Thessalonians 2:3), and (for some interpreters) 'the beast' (Revelation 13:1–10); but his ultimate overthrow is assured (Revelation 19:19–20; 21:10).

While Jesus offered hope to all, he was also clear about the destiny of unbelievers (e.g. John 3:36), saying they would end up in life's rubbish dump, *Gehenna*, usually translated 'hell' but in fact Jerusalem's rubbish dump in Jesus' day. Some see hell as a place of eternal punishment, but others see it as a place of utter destruction. Whichever it is, Jesus said it should be avoided at all costs (Mark 9:43–48).

What Happens After Death?

Death isn't the opposite of life; it's the opposite of birth. It's the moment, Jesus said, when believers leave their body and immediately enter God's dimension. That's why he promised the man crucified alongside him, '*Today* you will be with me in paradise' (Luke 23:43) – no delay, purgatory, reincarnation or soul-sleep; simply being 'with Christ, which is far better' (Philippians 1:23).

Heaven: Not Our Final Home!

While Christians often speak about 'spending eternity in heaven', that's not actually what the Bible says. The ultimate destination is spending eternity with God *on earth*. Heaven is simply a beautiful waiting room until Jesus returns. When he does, he will bring his followers with him, equipped with 'resurrection bodies' (Romans 8:23; 1 Corinthians 15:35–57), to spend eternity on a renewed and perfect earth (Revelation 21:1 – 22:5).

IMAGES OF HEAVEN
Because the Bible doesn't provide many details about the future life, artists have used their imagination to portray it, often reflecting the age in which they lived. This stained glass window from St Vitus Cathedral, Prague, portrays it as a happy, beautiful place.

KEY SAYING

'Be prepared, because you do not know what day your Lord is coming.'
MATTHEW 24:42

121

His Revelation
THINGS AREN'T ALWAYS WHAT THEY SEEM

Jesus' final words are found, not in the Gospels, but in Revelation. The apostle John, exiled to Rome's penal colony on Patmos, suddenly heard an unexpected yet familiar voice. Turning round, he saw Jesus (1:9–18). The last time he'd seen him was sixty years earlier; but now Jesus, kind as ever, had come to answer his questions: Why all this persecution? How long before God did something? Jesus gave John a behind-the-scenes tour, sweeping from his day into eternity, where he saw Jesus controlling history, steering it towards its climax. Things really weren't what they seemed to be after all, as Revelation shows.

To ensure letters weren't tampered with, they were sealed with wax. John sees the scroll of history, sealed with seven seals (that is, absolutely secure), which only Jesus can open (Revelation 5:1 – 8:1). He alone makes sense of history and knows its destiny.

Approaches to Revelation

There are several different approaches to Revelation, but they fall into three main types:

■ **Preterist:** ('relating to the past'): everything described or prophesied was fulfilled in the first century AD (the view of the early church).

■ **Futurist:** while some events were fulfilled in the first century, most will happen at the End (a view developed in the nineteenth and twentieth centuries).

■ **Idealist:** the events are symbolic of timeless truths – the triumph of good over evil (Augustine's view).

Opposition to Christianity

While Christianity was just another Jewish sect, and therefore a *religio licta* (state-authorized religion), Rome was happy to leave it alone. But once they saw it as a breakaway religion, their hostility grew; and that hostility became persecution when emperors started claiming divinity and Christians refused to worship them, rejecting their claims to be 'son of a god' and 'saviour of the world', titles they reserved for Jesus alone. They were persecuted terribly therefore, particularly by Nero (AD 54–68) and Domitian (AD 81–96), as many Christians have been over the past 2,000 years. This was the background to Revelation.

The 50,000-seater Colosseum (Flavian Amphitheatre) in Rome where many Christians were thrown to wild animals or forced to fight gladiators.

Keys to Revelation

Revelation can be a puzzling book, but remembering three things helps our interpretation:

■ **It is a *revelation*:** its very name showing Jesus wanted to *reveal* things not *hide* them. It isn't a puzzle for decoding the date of Jesus' return but God revealing a simple truth: there is a battle going on and Christians therefore sometimes suffer; but Satan is defeated and his ultimate end is assured.

■ **It is *apocalyptic*:** a well-known literary genre using pictures, symbols and numbers. While we find this difficult, John's first readers would have easily understood it. The key is always asking, 'How would John's first readers have understood this?'

■ **It is a *letter*:** sent to seven churches in Asia Minor (modern Turkey) to encourage them in the face of persecution. Whatever it might say about the future, its primary purpose was to bring immediate hope to *them*.

> *The reason the Son of God appeared was to destroy the devil's work.*
> 1 JOHN 3:8

Revelation's Structure

Revelation is structured around the number 'seven':

■ **Introduction:** Jesus comes to encourage John (1:1–20).

■ **Seven letters:** Jesus dictates letters to churches in Asia Minor (2:1 – 3:22).

■ **Seven seals:** Jesus, enthroned in heaven, opens history's scroll (4:1 – 8:1).

■ **Seven trumpets:** God warns the world (8:2 – 11:19).

■ **Seven battles:** Satan attempts to destroy Jesus and God's people, but God protects them (12:1 – 15:4).

■ **Seven bowls:** God judges the world (15:5 – 16:21).

■ **Seven visions of Babylon's fall:** 'Babylon' (Rome or Judaism) crumbles (17:1 – 19:10).

■ **Seven visions of Jesus' victory:** Satan's downfall and the final judgment (19:1 – 21:4).

■ **Conclusion:** God's new creation (21:5 – 22:21).

The Millennium

Revelation speaks of Jesus reigning for 1,000 years (Revelation 20:1–7), but Christians have different views of this:

■ **Post-millennial:** a literal 1,000 years, *climaxing* in Jesus' return.

■ **Pre-millennial:** a literal 1,000 years, *beginning* with Jesus' return, when Satan is temporarily bound until Jesus' final coming.

■ **A-millennial:** a symbolic period signifying the time between Jesus' first and second comings.

The plain of Megiddo, where empires make their final stand against God (Revelation 16:16). Many battles happened here in Israel's history, but in a book so full of symbols, John may have meant this battle symbolically rather than literally.

Numbers in Revelation

Remembering that apocalyptic literature used numbers in very familiar ways helps our understanding of Revelation:

■ **7 = perfection, God's number** (from God resting on Day Seven after completing his perfect world). Seven churches symbolize God's whole church.

■ **6 = near-perfection, mankind's number** (from mankind's creation on Day Six). The Beast's number, therefore, is '666' (Revelation 13:18). No matter how hard he tries, he'll never reach 'seven'. He's only ever man, never God.

■ **3½ = half of seven, incomplete.** Three and a half years of suffering, therefore (Revelation 11), is bad but limited.

■ **10 = completeness.** 1,000 = 10x10x10 = absolutely complete. One thousand years (Revelation 20:4) is God's complete and appointed time.

■ **12 = God's people** (from Israel's twelve tribes). The twenty-four elders (Revelation 4:4) = 12 leaders of Israel + 12 apostles of the church, symbolizing God's entire people throughout history.

Sometimes numbers are combined. So 144,000 isn't the precise number in heaven (Revelation 7:4), but a combination of 12s and 10s: 12x12 (all God's people) x 10x10x10 (absolutely complete) = 144,000 = all God's people. Not one of them is missing!

Ancient catacombs (burial chambers) in Rome, where Christians met in secret. The ground beneath the city was honeycombed with tunnels from quarrying and digging sewers, and Jews had begun to bury their dead here. When Rome persecuted the Christians, they were driven underground and met in these catacombs. Secret signs, like the fish, marked their meeting places.

His Presence

FINDING JESUS TODAY

Each of the Gospels finishes open-endedly: Matthew has Jesus sending his disciples into the world; Mark has the women discovering Jesus is risen; Luke has Jesus returning to heaven; John has Jesus recommissioning Peter. None tells us any more nor answers further questions. But this was no accident; they meant to end like that. It was their way of saying that, through his followers in whom he lived and whose lives he changed, the story of Jesus continued. Two thousand years later, Christians are still claiming the same.

What is a Christian?

Jesus made it clear again and again that knowing God isn't about being born into a particular family, people or culture, but about experiencing a new relationship through a new spiritual birth (John 3:1–16) and then following Jesus on a daily basis. Being a follower of Jesus inevitably involves believing what Jesus believed, accepting what he said about:

■ **Himself:** that he was no one less than God himself;

■ **His purpose:** that he came to die on the cross to pay for our sins;

■ **His challenge:** that he calls us to live a life that is pleasing to God and helpful to others;

■ **His people:** that he is gathering a new people who live together as an expression of God's kingdom;

■ **His hope:** that through him, death is not the end; there is a heaven to be gained and a hell to be avoided.

Christians don't claim to be perfect or 'goodie-goodies'; they simply claim that a very real change has happened in them and that an adventure in life with Jesus has begun.

Many churches light candles as a reminder that Jesus, the Light of the World, is present with them.

The statue of Christ the Redeemer towering over the city of Rio de Janeiro, his arms outstretched as a sign of blessing to all.

'We would like to see Jesus.'
JOHN 12:21

● SEE ALSO
CAN WE FIND THE REAL JESUS? P. 8
DISCIPLESHIP P. 40
TRUSTING THE GOSPELS PP. 8–9

Changed Lives

I sometimes present BBC faith programmes, which has caused me to meet some amazing people. What always strikes me is the very varied backgrounds they come from, yet all are convinced that Jesus in his kindness came looking for them (often when they weren't looking for him) and changed their lives. Some of those guests have included:

■ A woman who became a high-class prostitute to support her children. She was attracted to Christianity by the practical, non-judgmental help Christians gave her, setting her on a journey of discovery that changed her life.

■ A young man whose fascination with automatic writing led to powerful and frightening demonic experiences but who was freed and transformed through the prayer of a Christian friend.

■ A Rwandan refugee whose family had been murdered but who found inner peace through discovering Jesus' message of loving your enemies.

■ A lady with chronic rheumatoid arthritis who was instantly healed by the Jesus she hated, and who was so melted by his kindness that she became a Christian there and then.

■ An atheistic philosopher whose studies led him to the conclusion that only Jesus' philosophy made sense of life. He went on to become one of Britain's leading professors of philosophy.

Of course, the classic argument is to dismiss such people as weak and needing a crutch. But Christians believe this is an argument that simply doesn't hold water. Of course some who become Christians may be weak (just like some atheists or agnostics may be weak); but many successful, fulfilled, intelligent people become Christians too, claiming they simply recognized truth when they saw it and found even more fulfilment and purpose in sharing their life with Jesus. That's why the guests on my programmes have included two leading Oxford professors, both world-class experts in their field, a former British government advisor, leading specialists in ecology, finance, business and science, as well as lots of 'ordinary' people. All these would reject assertions of their faith being a crutch, but rather claim it 'works' and that Jesus can still give meaning and change lives today as much as he was doing 2,000 years ago.

Help on the Journey

Jesus promised he wouldn't leave his followers alone (John 14:18), and Christians believe that this promise still holds true today. So whether we are searching for him for the first time or have been following him for years, we can be sure he actually wants to help us find him. Some of the things he provides to help us do that include:

■ **The Bible:** for Christians, not just a history book, but God's book of truth and revelation, inspired by his Holy Spirit. For someone searching for Jesus, the Bible is probably the best place to begin, especially the four Gospels that tell his story and record his teaching.

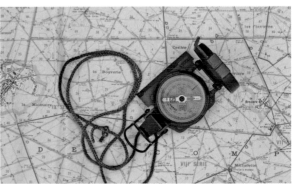

■ **The church:** by no means perfect (because it's made up of people just like us!) but still a good place to find help on the journey and answers to our questions. Church comes in a wide variety of expressions, from liturgical to informal, from big to small; so there's something for everyone, whatever their character, style or taste.

■ **The Holy Spirit:** the one Jesus promised he would send to guide us into all truth (John 16:13). That's why Christians believe we can ask the Holy Spirit to help us in both our search for Jesus and our continued journey of faith.

For all who are serious about finding and following Jesus, he made a promise: 'I will come to you' (John 14:18). Countless millions still find that promise to be true today and find that the presence of this amazing man – God become man – truly makes a difference.

KEY SAYING

'I am the Living One; I was dead, and behold I am alive for ever and ever!'

REVELATION 1:18

Index

Picture acknowledgments

Alamy: p. 14t Dennis Cox; pp. 16, 33t, 35b, 98bl PhotoStock-Israel; pp. 18 (both images), 26ml, 31r, 42b, 48, 62l, 70l, 108r, 123t Israel Images; pp. 30l, 72t Eitan Simanor; p. 42t Hanan Isachar; p. 44l Wendy White; p. 45 Images&Stories; p. 49bl Nir Alon; p. 51t Martin Harvey; pp. 51b, 111t imagebroker; p. 54t Mark Boulton; p. 55t Ivan Vdovin; p. 55b Mary Evans Picture Library; p. 64 StockImages; p. 75m Helene Rogers; p. 76br Michele Falzone; p.88t Geomphotography; p. 88b Eniz Umuler; p.89 Paul Bucknall/Ark Religion.com; p. 94l ASP Religion; p. 96t Daily Grind; pp. 96b, 98tr The Print Collector; p. 99t Catriona Bass; p.108l David Pearson; p. 111b Cephas Picture Library; p. 112r Adrian Sherratt; p. 114 Borderlands; p. 121tl Dave Penman

Art Archive: p. 77tr Musée du Louvre Paris/Gianni Dagli Orti; p. 84 Saint Sebastian Chapel Lanslevillard Savoy/ Gianni Dagli Orti; p.85 National Museum La Valletta Malta/Gianni Dagli Orti

Corbis: pp. 12b Sandro Vannini; pp. 13t, 23t Buddy Mays; pp. 19t, 34, 94r, 97t Dave Bartruff; p. 20 Peter M. Wilson; p. 21bl Peter Turnley; p. 22t Gianni Dagli Orti; pp. 23m, 103r The Gallery Collection; p. 24 Ralph A. Clevenger; pp. 25, 27l, 46, 49t, 87 (both images), 91 Hanan Isachar; pp. 27tr, 29t Ted Spiegel; pp. 28l, 58b, 60, 63b, 99b, 118 Richard T. Nowitz; p. 33b Dave G. Houser; p. 35t Shai Ginott; p. 36 P Deliss/Godong; p.37t John Heseltine; p. 37b Herbert Spichtinger; pp. 38t, 119b Roger Ressmeyer; p. 38b Matthew Polak; p. 39r B. Lawton/photocuisine; pp. 39l, 82bl Francis G. Mayer; p. 41t Tibor Bognar; p. 43l A. Inden; p. 44br Emmanuel Kwitema/Reuters; p. 56t Joseph Sohm; p. 56b Jim Richardson; p. 57 Ronen Zvulun/Reuters; p. 58t Wolfram Steinberg/dpa; p. 61t Burstein Collection; pp.62r, 80 , 92 Brooklyn Museum; p. 67t Dr. John C. Trever, Ph. D.; p. 69t Viviane Moss; p. 69b Flip Schulke; p.70r Joe McDonald; p.71bl Yossan; p. 72bl Corbis; p. 73 Shannon Stapleton/Reuters; p. 75tl Bojan Brecelj; p. 75tr Werner Forman; p. 76l Marc Garanger; p. 82m Elio Ciol; p.82br Erik de Castro; p. 86 Summerfield Press; p. 90 Stapleton Collection; p. 95 Ed Young/AgStock Images; p. 97m Pascal Deloche/Godong; p.97br Lucas Jackson/ Reuters; p.104r Bernd Kohlhas; pp. 105t, 107 Reuters; p. 106 Stefano Bianchetti; p. 109 Philadelphia Museum of Art; p.112tl Gaby Wojciech/Westend61;

p. 112bl Radius Images; p. 113l Kevin Fleming; p. 113r Robin Utrecht/Pool/ Reuters; p. 115 Hoberman Collection; p. 116t Julian Kumar/Godong; p. 116b Philippe Giraud/Sygma; p. 117r Bettman; p. 117m Hilgers/dpa; p. 117l Pelletier Micheline/Sygma; p. 119t Peter Adams; p. 120 John Lund; p. 121tr Image Source; p. 121b Gavin Hellier/Robert Harding World Imagery; p.122r Art on File; p. 123br Charles & Josette Lenars; p. 123bl Christine Mariner/Design Pics; p. 124t Kelly Redinger/Design Pics; p. 124b Dennis Degnan; p.125t moodboard

David Alexander: pp. 15mr, 17tr, 22bl,

Getty: p. 29b Henri Silberman; p. 59t Eitan Simanor; p. 61b Brian Hendler; pp. 66t, 83tr The Bridgeman Art Library; p. 68 John Chillingworth/Picture Post; p.71tr Vatican Pool; p. 74 Lisa Spindler Photography Inc.; p. 77bl Pankaj Shah; p. 78 Richard Passmore; p. 97bl Hans Neleman; p. 122l Nick Dolding

iStock: pp. 50, 67b, 81

Mike Beaumont: p. 105b

Lion: pp. 9 (both images), 15tr, 26b, 31l, 35m, 41br, 43r, 47, 65, 83bl, 98br, 110

Nicholas Rous: pp. 10t, 41bl, 52b, 125b

Peter Walker: p. 28r

Photolibrary: p. 17mr Mick Rock; p. 21tr E&E Image Library; p. 23b The Print Collector; p. 40 Joel Salcido; p. 53 Eitan Simanor; p. 54b The British Library

Topfoto: p. 59b The Granger Collection; p. 66b The Image Works

Zev Radovan: pp. 8, 10b, 19b, 32, 49br, 52t, 63t, 79, 101tr, 101bl, 103, 104t

Maps and Illustrations

All maps and diagrams by **Richard Watts**, unless listed below.

Julie Baines: p. 9t

Dick Barnard: p. 17cl

Simon Emery: p. 14b, 101tl

Rex Nicholls: p. 101br

Lion Hudson

Commissioning editor: Kate Kirkpatrick

Project editor: Miranda Powell

Proofreader: Rachel Ashley-Pain

Book designer: Nicholas Rous

Jacket designer: Jonathan Roberts

Picture researcher: Jenny Ward

Production manager: Kylie Ord